Angel

TV Milestones

Series Editors

Barry Keith Grant
Brock University

Jeannette Sloniowski
Brock University

TV Milestones is part of the Contemporary Approaches to Film and Television Series

A complete listing of the books in this series can be found online at *wsupress.wayne.edu*

General Editor

Barry Keith Grant
Brock University

Advisory Editors

Patricia B. Erens
School of the Art Institute of Chicago

Robert J. Burgoyne
Wayne State University

Lucy Fischer
University of Pittsburgh

Tom Gunning
University of Chicago

Anna McCarthy
New York University

Caren J. Deming
University of Arizona

Peter X. Feng
University of Delaware

Lisa Parks
University of California–
Santa Barbara

ANGEL

Stacey Abbott

TV MILESTONES SERIES

Wayne State University Press   Detroit

Library of Congress Cataloging-in-Publication Data

Abbott, Stacey.
Angel / Stacey Abbott.
p. cm.
Includes bibliographical references and index.
ISBN 978-0-8143-3319-8 (pbk. : alk. paper)
1. Angel (Television program : 1999–2004) I. Title.
PN1992.77.A527A33 2009
791.45'72—dc22
2008052058

For Simon—my partner in life and love

CONTENTS

ACKNOWLEDGMENTS

First and foremost I would like to thank Joss Whedon, David Boreanaz, and the team of creators who brought their vision for *Angel* to the screen between 1999 and 2004. Thank you for the entertainment and the inspiration over the years. I would like to thank Wayne State University Press for supporting this project and recognizing that *Angel* is a true milestone in television history. Thanks in particular to Annie Martin for all of her assistance throughout this process and to the readers of the manuscript for their insight and guidance. I am indebted to Roehampton University and the Arts and Humanities Research Council for funding my sabbatical to write this book as well as a research trip to the New York Library of the Performing Arts. The year 2006 was truly unforgettable. A special thanks goes to the film team at Roehampton who had to carry a heavy workload while I was on leave. I owe a further debt to my office and conference buddy, Deborah Jermyn, for her endless support, not to mention for telling me about the TV Milestones series in the first place. You are a true friend and scholar. Special thanks to the staff at the Billy Rose Theatre Collection at the New York

Library of the Performing Arts for all their help—in particular for the endless photocopying. The staff of the British Film Institute's National Library deserves particular acknowledgment for all of their hard work over the years in making all of my research easy and pleasurable. I would like to thank Rhonda V. Wilcox and David Lavery for inviting me to be the keynote speaker at the Slayage Conference at Gordon College in Barnesville, Georgia, in 2006. This was a great opportunity to discuss some of the ideas explored in this book, and the feedback I received was very helpful. Thanks to everyone at the conference for sharing their ideas about *Buffy* and *Angel,* and especially for my Mr. Pointy. I owe a special thanks to Rhonda and David for their encouragement over the years. Thank you to all who attended the *Buffy Hereafter* conference in Istanbul and provided incredibly useful feedback to my work. I would also like to thank Denzell Richards for his help preparing clips for both of these conferences, as well as his shared enthusiasm for *Angel.* To Bronwen Calvert and Lorna Jowett, fellow *Angel* scholars and fans, I extend my thanks for sharing and exchanging so many exciting ideas about *Angel.* Our regular chats about the show are incredibly stimulating. As always, I owe a debt to my family for their love, especially to my husband, Simon, who has been an inspiration and a support throughout this project. You are my partner in everything and so it is to you that I dedicate this book.

"A Seminal Show Canceled by the Idiot Networks"

> Denver: A vampire wanting to slay a
> demon in order to help some grubby
> humans? I just don't get it.
> Angel: To be honest—I'm not sure I do
> either.
>
> *"Are You Now or Have You Ever Been"*
> (2:2)

It is apparent that following the broadcast of the first episode of *Angel*, the spin-off to the successful teen series *Buffy the Vampire Slayer* (1997–2003), on October 5, 1999, that Denver was not alone in his confusion. Some of the critics didn't "get it" either. Marvin Kitman suggested that the series' creators, Joss Whedon and David Greenwalt, "have had a bad case of tired blood, brought on by watching too many reruns of *Forever Knight*," claiming that the new series is just "an excuse to suck the blood out of *Buffy*" (1999). Steve Parks complained that Angel, the title character, "is too dour to crack jokes" (1999), a concern shared by Diane Werts who, while reviewing the show's opening episode favorably, argued that "to really take a bite out of the prime-time ratings" *Angel* needed to loosen up and "go at life with gusto" and not just guilt (1999). Other critics, however, did "get it." Matt Roush described *Angel* as "sleek and sexy in its Gothic gloom" (1999); Michele Greppi noted that "if *Buffy the Vampire Slayer* is about high school as hell, *Angel* is going to be a post-graduate course on coming to grips with life not as you dreamed it but as it unfolds" (1999); and Joyce Millman pointed to the irony in the fact that "some of TV's most moving and astute meditations on what it is to be human come from a show about a guy who's undead" (2001, 30).

More important, the fans "got it." While never commanding the audience figures of its parent show, *Angel* developed a loyal following—so loyal that when the series was canceled in 2004 they launched a highly public campaign to save it. Bearing the slogan "Looking for a Few (Million) Good Viewers? We'll Follow Angel to Hell . . . or Another Network," this crusade took the forms of online petitions, telephone and postcard campaigns to the networks and advertisers, ads in *Variety* and *Hollywood Reporter,* a live rally in Los Angeles in conjunction with a worldwide online rally, and the infamous Angelmobile—a mobile billboard in L.A. In order to truly convey the fans' commitment to the show, the campaign also demonstrated a complete engagement with the themes of the series by raising funds for the Red Cross, running blood drives (yes, blood), and donating money to the Los Angeles Regional Food Bank. While in the end the attempt to save the show was unsuccessful, the fans had demonstrated their loyalty to the ethos of the series by choosing to mirror Angel's mission and "help the helpless."

Angel from Conception to Cancellation

Angel was produced by Twentieth Century Fox and broadcast on the WB (Warner Brothers) from 1999 to 2004. Designed as a spin-off of *Buffy,* the series was the brainchild of *Buffy* creator and executive producer Joss Whedon and producer David Greenwalt. Following the success of Angel's unexpected turn to evil in season two of *Buffy*, Whedon realized that there was untapped scope to this character—and the acting ability of David Boreanaz—that might best be explored through his own series (Malcolm 2004, 22). When approached to run the show, Greenwalt leaped at the opportunity and immediately suggested that the often-comic character of wealthy, superficial, and acerbic Cordelia Chase (Charisma Carpenter) join the new series as a brighter balance to Angel's darkness (Nazzaro 2002, 156). With this decision the fundamental premise of the series was established. The show would follow the departure of Angel (David Boreanaz), Buffy's soulful vampire-lover, from Sunnydale at the end of *Buffy* season three as he arrives in Los Angeles and, along with the now impoverished Cordelia, sets up his own demon-fighting operation. The choice of L.A. provided the broad metaphor for the series, which was that "LA [is] a place that people come to in order to start over" (Greenwalt, cited in Nazzaro 2002, 157).

The iconic image of Angel from "City Of."

To aid Angel on his mission, a team of demon-hunters, presented as the more grown up and damaged version of *Buffy*'s team of teenage vampire hunters, were gradually built up over the series' five-year run. Each member of this team carries the burden of his or her own past, insecurities, personal failings, and transgressions and is, like Angel, looking for some form of redemption. The team of Angel Investigations (AI) is made up of Francis Doyle (Glenn Quinn), Wesley Wyndam-Pryce (Alexis Denisof), Charles Gunn (J. August Richards), Winifred "Fred" Burkle (Amy Acker), Lorne (Andy Hallett), and Spike (James Marsters).

Angel's life on the WB network was, however, often as fraught as his life on the streets of L.A. While the basic premise of the show was established early on, the series underwent a few reboots before the writers settled on the series' main concerns, narrative approach, and broad themes, satisfying their own ambitions for the show as well as the desires of the network. Early drafts of the first few episodes presented *Angel* as a "dark, gritty urban show" featuring undercover police, drugs, and prostitution, causing the more family-/teen-oriented network to back off the project (Greenwalt, cited in Nazzaro 2002, 157). Whedon and Greenwalt agreed to change their conception of the series and transformed this more "realistic" approach into a more fantastical exploration of darkness and evil. L.A. remained central but less as a real place and more as a noirish urban conurbation in which the lonely and vulnerable are preyed upon by monsters, both human and demonic (see Jacob 2005). The second reboot came during the first season. The show was originally supposed to be an episodic series with the detective agency at the center and Angel working for a new client and facing a different demon every week. Even the evil law firm of Wolfram & Hart, conceived from the start as a corporate opposition to Angel in keeping with the show's big-city setting, was supposed to introduce a different lawyer every episode, reinforcing its position as a faceless form of evil. This approach did make the series very different from its parent show, *Buffy the Vampire Slayer*, well-known at this point for its seasonal arc narratives. Halfway through the first season, however, this changed and the series became increasingly focused on Angel's character and the narrative conflict between Angel and Wolfram & Hart, now regularly represented by recurring characters Lindsey McDonald (Christian Kane), Lilah Morgan (Stephanie Romonov), and Holland Manners (Sam Anderson).

Whedon resolutely argues that the change came naturally to them as he and Greenwalt became less interested in the episodic cases and increasingly drawn to Angel's story (Malcolm 2004, 24). The fact, however, that ratings for the first season were dramatically lower than those for *Buffy* had been may have also contributed to the decision to reorient the series to a more familiar and successful narrative structure. Clearly the choice to program *Angel* directly after *Buffy* was made with an aim to carry the audience over from one series to the other, as were strategic crossover episodes such as "I Will Remember You" (1:8) and "Five by Five" (1:18) that linked the two narratives together, cleverly programmed for sweeps weeks to maximize the ratings. While this served to consolidate the ratings enough to ensure a second season and an increase in budget and production values (most visible through the move from the small and claustrophobic AI offices in season one to the grand and stately Hyperion Hotel in season two), ratings continued to be a major issue for the show. According to Phil Colvin, these strategies did enable the series to maintain consistent audience figures by developing a loyal fandom nationally and internationally, but in the long term *Angel* failed to gain the necessary upside to these figures that guarantee a show's success (2005, 17–30).

This uncertainty about the show's future was further hampered when it lost its strong lead-in in 2001 following

Buffy's acrimonious departure from the WB. The impact of this event on *Angel* was twofold. First, *Angel*'s future at the WB was unclear. Much conjecture in the industry press questioned whether the network would cancel *Angel* in retaliation for its loss of *Buffy*,[1] and the show's connection to the more established series was perceived to be responsible for its steady audience figures in its first two seasons. Second, no longer part of a solid lineup, the show was repeatedly moved around, sometimes broadcast opposite very popular series like *The Bachelor* or in tandem with seemingly incompatible series like the "goody-goody drama" *7th Heaven* (WB, 1996–2007) (Millman 2001, 21). This turbulent relationship with the WB continued up until the end of season four when, after much speculation and anticipation, the network confirmed it would be renewing the series for a fifth season. It had agreed to this, however, with a few provisos: with the finale of *Buffy the Vampire Slayer* (now broadcast on UPN) having just aired, the WB announced that the phenomenally popular character Spike (James Marsters) would join *Angel* the following season; the budget for season five was effectively cut;[2] and after a climatic fourth season that had taken narrative arcs to its ultimate extreme, the writers agreed to return the show to a more episodic/case-of-the-week formula, a strategy that seemed to be more inviting to the uninitiated audience member (Gross 2003a). Despite these conditions, however, tensions with the WB finally came to a head in season five when questions about the series' future were finally answered on February 13, 2004, with the announcement that the show was canceled.

Angel as TV Milestone

Throughout its turbulent life on the WB, *Angel*, aimed at the older demographic of twenty-five- to thirty-five-year-olds, was envisaged by its creators, Joss Whedon, David Greenwalt, and the writing team of Mutant Enemy, as a darker meditation on how to be human in a corrupt and violent world. While a spin-off to the successful *Buffy the Vampire Slayer*, the creators' approach to the show was more in keeping with such notable and unique spin-offs as *Rhoda* (CBS, 1974–78) and *Lou Grant* (CBS, 1977–82), rather than the repetition of formula that characterizes more recent series like *CSI: Miami* (CBS, 2002–) and *CSI: New York* (CBS, 2004–), and the numerous spin-offs of *Law and Order* (NBC, 1990–).[3] While drawing on the success of parent series the *Mary Tyler Moore Show* (1970–77), *Rhoda,* and *Lou Grant* were unique shows with their own style, comedy, and narrative approaches dictated by the series' title characters. Similarly, the approach to *Angel* was to create a distinct series with its own clear identity rather than simply repeat the formula of *Buffy*. While *Buffy the Vampire Slayer* used the monster as metaphor to explore the horrors of growing up, *Angel* addressed the horrors of adulthood. While *Buffy* chronicled the times in young adult lives when strength can be found in family and friends, *Angel* explored the rifts and tensions that develop between family and friends. While *Buffy* looked to the future, *Angel* reflected on the past and its often painful impact on the present. As Tim Minear, a writer and eventual executive producer for the series, explains, "a show called *Angel*, about a guy who ate his parents and is a vampire and killed a bunch of people, you know it's gonna have its dark side. And if you can't do that dark side, you don't have a show" (qtd. in Bratton 2000). That darkness was manifested in the series' noirish urban location as well as through the representation of corporate corruption in the form of the evil law firm Wolfram & Hart. More important, it is present in Angel himself as he constantly negotiates the moral ambiguities of his own existence as a vampire cursed with the return of his soul and now haunted by the atrocities he has committed in his 250 years as a vampire. Furthermore, he is a vampire who must live with the dark side that is an integral part of himself and from which he gains much of his strength. While on *Buffy,*

Angel, primarily written as a love interest for the series' main character, was a cipher for Buffy's teenage insecurities, desires, and awakening passions. In his own series, however, he became a complex character able to explore the nuances of his good and evil ways. As David Boreanaz explained, it is "the ability to integrate the good and bad sides" that attracted him to the character of Angel: "[t]hat is what I want to bring to the series, a character that could go both ways, that can play both kinds of faces" (qtd. in Persons 1999, 11).

What stands out about *Angel* is its commitment to exploring dark and morally ambiguous themes, enhanced by the show's irreverent humor, the flouting of generic conventions, and an emphasis on a cinematic visual style. Chapter 1 will explore how *Angel* has made its mark in television by first addressing the collaborative authorship of the writing team at Mutant Enemy as a means of challenging the single auteurist framework that has marked much of the work on *Buffy the Vampire Slayer* and *Angel*. This will be followed by a discussion in chapter 2 of the series' experimentation with genre hybridity, conveyed through the show's near cinematic visual style, while chapter 3 will position the show as an example of TV horror at a time when the attitudes toward horror on television are in a state of flux. Chapter 4 will address the significant role that masculinity plays within the narrative matrix of *Angel* with a particular focus on the representation of male friendship. In chapter 5 I will conclude my discussion of the series with case studies of three individual episodes that demonstrate how *Angel* experimented with the conventions of television, aesthetically, narratively, and generically. Through these discussions I will demonstrate that to truly "get" *Angel* you have to be open to its unique interplay, both visually and narratively, between light and dark, comedy and horror, in which the boundaries between good and evil, man and monster, life and death, are repeatedly blurred, for Angel—the *vampire* with a *soul*—embodies it all.

"Grrr Aaargh!"
The Collective Vision
of Mutant Enemy

You look at any television show that is at
all memorable and anything that's really
good, like *The X-Files* or *Buffy,* you'll see
that they are created by writers, Chris
Carter or Joss Whedon, David Kelly. These
guys have a vision and the people that produce television are the writers. Whenever
you see "executive producer," it generally
means the top writer on a TV show. And
we do more than just write the shows, we
cast them, we work with the production
people, we produce the shows. All the way
through the post-production, from editing,
to the mix, to the sound effects, to the
music, all that stuff. We're there every step
of the way. . . . In movies, it ain't like that.

Tim Minear (qtd. in Bratton 2000)

Joss Whedon, creator of *Buffy the Vampire Slayer*, *Angel,*
Firefly (2002), and *Dollhouse* (2009) is one of the leading
names within a new generation of television writer-producers who, according to Roberta Pearson, had "control over the
day-to-day running of the show" but with "relative freedom
from the demands of studios and networks" (2005, 17, 18).

As such the creative vision for these series is generally attributed to Whedon. David Lavery argues that unlike many other television series, "it is not at all difficult . . . to locate the author of *Buffy the Vampire Slayer*. As its creator, executive producer, writer/co-writer . . . Joss Whedon is, beyond question, the 'mad genius' . . . of *Buffy*" (2002, 252). Lavery argues that it is Whedon's dominant input into the series' creation as a producer, writer, and director that makes him the primary author of the show. Similarly, in interviews cast and crew of both *Buffy* and *Angel* regularly credit Whedon with being the creative force behind each of these series. For instance, David Greenwalt, co-creator of *Angel*, clearly points out that "any story that you see on *Buffy* or *Angel* has been broken substantially by Mr. Whedon, if not entirely" (qtd. in Nazzaro 2002, 154),[1] while in another interview Greenwalt argues that Whedon's hard work and talent serve as an inspiration to the team for "[e]very year he sets some huge new challenge for himself and it raises the bar for all of us. It's helpful to see the guy at the top working that hard and stretching that far and that's what makes a well-rounded production" (qtd. in Bratton 2002). Rhonda V. Wilcox, however, specifically attributes Whedon's "genius" to his ability "to work with a cast and crew of high quality . . . [and] bring out the best in those he works with" (2005, 6). While Wilcox is speaking of everyone involved in the creation of *Buffy,* her comment quite aptly applies to the writing team at Mutant Enemy who worked alongside Whedon in the development of each television series. As Whedon himself explains, "I've spent five years culling the most extraordinary staff, which I trust to share my vision and my experience. So if somebody gets it right, I leave it alone" (qtd. in Nazzaro 2002, 227). It is therefore to this team of writers specifically working on *Angel* that I turn my attention.

In film production, the director is usually perceived to be the creative force behind a film despite the fact that film is a collaborative medium. This is based on the understanding that it is usually the responsibility of the director to oversee the contributions of writers, cinematographers, sound technicians, composers, actors, and editors and pull together this range of creative input into one coherent vision. In American television, the structure is very different for, as indicated by Tim Minear in the passage that opens this chapter, a writer is usually at the helm of a TV series and is responsible for its overall conception.[2] More to the point, a team of writers work together to create the show. Minear may credit top writers like Whedon, Carter, and Kelly for their vision, but the "we" in his statement applies to the contribution made by the entire team. While it is the responsibility of executive producer–writers like Whedon and Greenwalt to establish the vision for the series, the team of writers turn that vision into televisual reality. Under the supervision of the "showrunner," the most senior writer/producer on the series who oversees the writing and production of each episode, the writing team maps out the trajectory for each season, establishes pivotal narrative and character points, and pitches and breaks each individual episode with consideration for how it contributes to the overall narrative arc while ensuring that it works within its own four-act structure.

In addition, the more established writers on the team, promoted to the various levels of producer, take responsibility for more than writing. They are responsible for rewrites as well as making story-line decisions and commissioning scripts. They are also often involved in casting, editing, or the filming of their script (Nazzaro 2002, 8). This is a particularly significant part of the Mutant Enemy practice of mentoring its writers and promoting from within; as Steven DeKnight explains, writers at all levels, not just the senior staff, were given the opportunity to take a more significant creative role in the series: "On *Buffy* and *Angel*, even at the lower level, you get invited in to work on the bigger creative picture. The writers are often sent down to the sets to watch vital scenes—they are sent into the editing suite to help fix problems—we are often asked into casting—you don't get that on other shows where the writers are kept much more insular" (qtd. in Kaveney 2004b, 120). Furthermore, the vision for the series evolved through the collective contribution of the writers from year to year. A film may be a collective project supervised by one director, but a television series is an ever-changing entity and as such the vision evolves along with its writing team.

While Whedon was the primary creative force behind the conception of *Buffy the Vampire Slayer*, a role he maintained throughout the series' seven seasons, his relationship to *Angel* was quite different. The character of Angel was born out of *Buffy* and the series does exist within Whedon's vision for his universe, but the show's initial conception grew out of his creative collaboration with David Greenwalt. Whedon took on the position of executive producer on *Angel* and made a significant contribution to the series, but Greenwalt took on the role of showrunner, a position handed over to Jeffrey Bell for seasons four and five following Greenwalt's departure. As such, the creative responsibility for the show was already split between the two senior writer-producers as Whedon explains.

> David is working mostly on *Angel*, I'm working mostly on *Buffy* and we're sort of supporting each other. We're constantly going back to each other's offices and stuff. I'm around the production of *Buffy* more and David is around the production of *Angel*. But in terms of breaking of stories, editing and all that stuff—that's happening together. The staff from both shows know each other and so there's a lot of cross currents, and we just sort of, you know, keep it as one big concept instead of two separate ones. (qtd. in Mauceri 2000, 10)

Furthermore, as Whedon began to develop a third television series to be produced by Mutant Enemy, *Firefly*, his hands-on involvement within *Angel* became somewhat more distant. Steven DeKnight explains that this gave the writing team of *Angel* a great deal of "flexibility because Joss, despite loving the show, has priorities elsewhere. He gives us the broad general idea or sometimes we pitch him the general idea and then he'll approve the final product in stages. . . . We do most of the stuff ourselves" (qtd. in DiLullo 2003). In this manner *Angel* stands as an informative case study for the collaborative nature of television, for it was born out of the relationships, previously established on *Buffy the Vampire Slayer*, between Whedon and Greenwalt as well as senior *Buffy* writers Marti Noxon, David Fury, Doug Petrie, and Jane Espenson, all of whom contributed to the early episodes of the series. Subsequently the show also developed its own collaborative team of writers who spearheaded the show's trajectory over its five-year run, including Tim Minear, Jeffrey Bell, Jim Kouf, Mere Smith, Elisabeth Craft, Sarah Fain, Steven DeKnight, and Drew Goddard. As such, rather than simply give credit exclusively to Whedon for the series' strengths and innovations, I intend to explore the collective creativity of the team of writers, drawn together in Whedon's production company Mutant Enemy, who serve at the helm of *Angel*.

As discussed in the introduction, the original intention was for *Angel* to be a gritty and episodic series in which Angel, acting as guardian for Los Angeles, fights different demons and monsters every week. However, the producers quickly realized that the primary point of interest for both the writers and the audience was its characters (Malcolm 2004, 24). As such, partway through the first season the narrative structure shifts from the monster of the week to episodes more focused on Angel's attempts to atone for his past as the evil vampire Angelus and his struggle to find redemption. This increasing focus on Angel's character arc led to the creation of a complex web of story lines, spanning from the late eighteenth to the early twenty-first century, that involved dramatic and often violent confrontations between friends and enemies from Angel's past and present. As Minear explains, the power of *Angel* was in its near operatic narrative structure that grew from season to season (cited in Gross 2003a, 56).

The complexity of the show is made all the more challenging by the fact that it was aired on a commercial network, running twenty-two episodes a year.[3] To produce this level of material involves a complex process of creativity within the highly structured industrial process that is American network television. The production schedule of any television series is intense. This was particularly the case on *Angel,* where, in addition to the dramatic interactions of its regular cast, each episode contained numerous locations, period costumes and sets, stunts, new demon/monster designs, musical performances, and special makeup and digital effects and took anywhere from four to six weeks to produce. While the writers were given six weeks prior to the start of overall production to begin writing the season's episodes, often allowing them up to two weeks to write an individual episode, by Christmas the writers had at best four to five days per script (Greenwalt 2003; Kaveney 2004b, 106). Furthermore, at any point in the season, various episodes would simultaneously be at different stages of the production process, writing, pre-production, filming, and editing, all of which would require the creative contributions of the writing team.[4]

The process of actually writing the scripts for *Angel* involved an intensively collaborative system. Each episode would generally begin as an idea pitched by the writers to Joss Whedon and David Greenwalt, who assisted in finessing it so that it fit within the overarching plans for the series and/or the specific season. Once an idea got the green light, the team would break the story as a group in the writers' room with the plan for the script broken down on a white board, act by act and scene by scene. In this process, the team worked out where the story was going, what role each character would play within the episode, where the key moments would be, and how to break up the episode into acts and then subsequently into scenes. Once this was done and then approved by Greenwalt and Whedon, a writer would be assigned to write an outline, followed by a first draft of the script. In most cases each script would go through a natural series of rewrites generally by the assigned writer, having received notes from Whedon and/or Greenwalt. Often, however, the showrunner or other senior writers would undertake rewrites where necessary and Greenwalt and Whedon would have final approval of the script. David Greenwalt explained, "[I]f we're lucky this [the script] will come in good. If we're not, it comes in not good. Then we all have to write and write and write and make it good" (Greenwalt 2003). Through these writing processes, as well as the fact that some scripts were deliberately cowritten because of time constraints or the need for specialist knowledge, any given episode, even where credited to one writer, could be the product of numerous creative voices and yet each episode had to uphold a unified vision and contribute to the series' overarching narrative.

Adding to the pressure of writing for *Angel*, each episode had to maintain narrative and character continuity not only with the other episodes in the series but also with the three preceding years of *Buffy the Vampire Slayer* as well as the narrative crossovers with *Buffy* in such episodes as "In the Dark" (1:3), "I Will Remember You" (1:8), "Five by Five" (1:18), "Sanctuary" (1:19), and "Darla" (2:7). Even when *Buffy* had moved to a different network, certain narrative continuities needed to be maintained between the two shows, including Angel's reaction and recovery from Buffy's death in "Heartthrob" (3:1), the revelation that she was in fact alive in

"Carpe Noctum" (3:4), Willow's arrival to help restore Angel's soul in "Orpheus" (4:15), and Faith's escape from jail and return to slayer duty in "Release" (4:14), which presages her return to Sunnydale in *Buffy* season seven. This narrative overlap requires a high level of coordination among scriptwriters, as well as the separate writing teams of *Buffy* and *Angel,* and accumulated knowledge of both shows. Tim Minear, who did not begin on *Buffy* like fellow writers David Greenwalt, Steven DeKnight, David Fury, and Drew Goddard, particularly credits the entire crew at Mutant Enemy for maintaining Buffy/Angelverse continuity as he explains, "We're pretty much making it up on the sly except there are continuity issues and luckily there are enough people at Mutant Enemy that have corporate memory so I don't have to know every episode backward and forward—they can tell me if I'm off" (Bratton 2000). This form of knowledge, however, applies to characterization as well as plot information. The writers not only maintained and developed the series' regulars from week to week in a coherent and believable fashion, they also ensured that crossover characters from *Buffy* were written in such a way as to be consistent with their earlier representations.

A particularly interesting case study that illustrates the complexity of the series' writing is the character Faith (Eliza Dushku), the murderous rogue slayer from Sunnydale who, having awakened from her coma in "This Year's Girl" (*B*4:15) and tormented Buffy in "Who Are You?" (*B*4:16), arrives in Los Angeles in "Five by Five" and is hired by Wolfram & Hart to kill Angel. In the first instance, this required *Angel*-writer Jim Kouf to write dialogue for a favorite character established on *Buffy* and maintain the rhythms and speech mannerisms that have come to be associated with this character. For instance, Faith's familiar use of false affection, established on *Buffy* through her loving references to Buffy as "B" or "Hey, girlfriend," are used in *Angel* to remind the audience of Faith and Angel's past together and to deliberately call to mind Faith's treacherous nature. Her opening line as she confronts Angel in his office and challenges him to "get in the game," "Hey, baby . . . come give us a hug," is deliberately reminiscent of her words to Buffy before the two slayers begin their fight to the death in "Graduation Day Part 1" (B3:21): "Ready to cut lose?" Faith asks Buffy. "Okay then—give us a kiss."

Furthermore, in "Five by Five" Faith maintains her use of sexualized language to convey her power and menace when she challenges Angel.

> Faith to Angel: What if you kill me and you experience your one true moment of pleasure—Oops. I'd get off on that. Go ahead—do me. Let's take that hellride together. Come on, Angel, I'm all yours. I'm giving you an open invitation. Jeez, you're pathetic. You and your little tortured soul. Gotta think everything through. Think fast, lover. If you don't do me, you know I'm going to do you.

While this episode upholds Faith's persona as the evil thrill seeker, the script also transforms that persona to suit the tone and atmosphere of *Angel* by presenting her as a darker and edgier version of *Buffy*'s Faith. Faith may have been a murderer on *Buffy* and was often described by the characters on that show as psychotic, but her turn to evil was a *choice* influenced by her anger at and envy of Buffy. The crimes she committed in Sunnydale, with the exception of the murder of the Mayor's assistant, which was an accident, were executed at the request of the season's Big Bad, the Mayor, or driven by revenge. While she clearly enjoyed her work, she never murdered for fun. When she arrives in Los Angeles, however, she is no longer looking for revenge nor is she working for anyone, at least not until she is hired by Wolfram & Hart and both revenge and monetary gain serve as incentives to kill

Angel. As such most of the crimes she commits, such as beating and robbing the pimp who tries to pick her up at the bus station, are committed to satisfy her own innate needs. She does them because she can and because it's fun. This is particularly evident in the nightclub scene where she starts a fight by seductively dancing with a man and then hitting his girlfriend in the face when she protests. The intention of this scene in its portrayal of Faith is evident in the episode's script. "And now fists and feet fly. With Faith in the middle of it. Enjoying the carefree moment of violence, grabbing one guy, punching the hell out of him, then slamming an elbow into someone else. This is a major free-for-all. Faith is out of control. Unleashing herself on everybody. And ROCKIN' TO THE MUSIC" (Kouf 2001).

18

Faith grooving to the music in "Five by Five."

The fight scene integrates Faith's fighting blows with her dance moves in a highly eroticized fashion that takes Faith's conflation of sexuality and violence further than ever portrayed on *Buffy*.[5] In this scene, there is no purpose to her actions; she is clearly positioned as out of control and acting on impulse.

Having slightly rewritten the character to suit the tone of *Angel*, the *Angel*-writers continued to develop Faith's characterization on the show as events within the Angelverse impact on her, making her unique among the characters from *Buffy* who crossed over to *Angel*. Oz, Willow, and Buffy may have visited Angel in L.A. but they returned to Sunnydale unchanged. In the case of Faith, however, her character underwent a major transformation. As Phil Colvin has argued, Faith's violence and sexuality on *Buffy* originally represented the dark potential of being a slayer, while on *Angel* she comes to represent the monster Angel once was (2005, 22). By the beginning of her second episode, therefore, Faith has recognized the monster she has become and has gone through an emotional breakdown that sets her on the same path to redemption as Angel ("Sanctuary"). As such Tim Minear and cowriter Joss Whedon found themselves in the position of having to write for a very different Faith than seen in earlier episodes, building on her character as previously written and taking her in a new direction. As Minear explains, "[I]n '5 by 5' Jim [Kouf] got to write wise cracking, evil Faith. By the time I got her she had the crap kicked out of her and I had to try to build her from a psychopath to somebody who wanted to change" (Bratton 2000).

The impact of this change to Faith's character is that there are fewer wise-cracking quips and she loses the confident, sexualized behavior and language that is here revealed to have been a mask for her self-loathing and insecurity. In fact, she says very little in the first half of the episode, described in the script as "unreadable," "blank," and "zombie-

Faith—beaten and broken in "Sanctuary."

girl" as Angel leads her to his apartment and puts her to bed to rest (Minear and Whedon 2001). When she does speak, her language becomes hesitant and her sentences broken as she struggles to control the pain and the remorse. In a confrontation with Buffy, Faith's delivery of this speech, with pauses and fractured sentences, conveys the lack of control that she is trying to describe.

> Faith to Buffy: And you can't stand that. You're all about control. You have no idea of what it's like on the other side—when nothing is in control—nothing makes sense. There's just pain, and hate, and nothing you do means anything. You can't even—[Buffy interrupts with a curt "Shut up"]. Just tell me how to make it better?

Changes to the character's behavior, language, and speech

mannerisms are used to convey her emotional evolution as written by the team of writers. This evolution continues through season four when Faith escapes from prison in order to save Angel ("Salvage"/"Release"/"Orpheus"). She returns as yet another version of Faith, now on the road to redemption and more secure in her identity than in "Sanctuary." We see a restoration of her confident, sexualized use of language as she tells Wesley that returning to vampire slaying is "just like riding a biker," and when facing Angelus for the first time she invites him to "come give us a kiss" ("Salvage," 4:13; written by David Fury). However, she also struggles to stay focused and not lose herself to her insecurities and anger. In "Release" (written by Steven DeKnight, Elizabeth Craft, and Sarah Fain), recovering from a severe beating, she stands in the shower, faces the camera in close-up and unleashes her anger and frustration by screaming and pummeling the wall. As a result, the character development that began in "Five by Five" and "Sanctuary" not only drew on her previous characterization on *Buffy* but also fed into later episodes on *Angel* and even *Buffy* as Faith leaves L.A. to return to Sunnydale for Buffy's final confrontation on the hellmouth. One of the characteristics of quality television, as defined by Robert J. Thompson, is "memory . . . these shows tend to refer back to previous episodes. Characters develop and change as the series goes on" (1996, 14). In *Angel* we see this type of memory carefully constructed and developed by the writing team of Angel, evolving across two television series and two teams of writers at Mutant Enemy.

The use of flashbacks in *Angel* further contributed to the complexity of its memory as the writers not only had to preserve continuity with the existing narratives of *Buffy* and *Angel*, but also developed Angel's two-hundred-and-fifty-year backstory. While flashbacks on *Buffy* were a rare occurrence, Whedon and his team preferring to focus on the Slayer's present circumstances, on *Angel* they became an integral strand

21

to the fabric of the series. With each season, new elements of this backstory were added, including Angel's life as Liam before becoming a vampire, his years with Darla (Julie Benz), the antagonistic relationship between Angelus, Darla, and the eighteenth-century vampire hunter Holtz (Keith Szarabajka), the Spike and Drusilla (Juliet Landow) years, and numerous post-ensoulment periods that demonstrated how Angel struggled between his vampire nature and his conscience. The gradual integration of the flashback structure into *Angel*'s narrative is a perfect example of something originating with Joss Whedon and then growing and developing into a major theme of the series through the contributions of *Angel*-writers like Tim Minear, Jim Kouf, David Greenwalt, Jeffrey Bell, and Mere Smith, each of whom have written one or more flashback episodes. The notion of creating a parallel between past and present events through the use of flashbacks in relation to Angel originated on *Buffy* in the penultimate episode of season two ("Becoming Part 1"; *B*2:21). Later in "Amends" (*B*3:10), the significance of Angel's past to his present is reinforced when his dreams and memories of past victims literally emerge into the present to torment him. Both episodes were written and directed by Joss Whedon.

On *Angel*, however, the flashback seemed to be the purview of Tim Minear, particularly in season one as he wrote "Somnambulist" (1:11) and "The Prodigal" (1:15), the first two episodes on *Angel* to feature flashbacks. The evolution of these episodes grew out of collaborative discussions among Whedon, Greenwalt, and Minear. In the case of "Somnambulist," the notion that "a vampire that Angel taught is killing in Angel's old M.O." originated with Greenwalt and Whedon, who put this episode idea to the staff writers at the start of the season for potential development (Minear, qtd. in Gross 2000a). Minear refashioned this concept by writing the opening act in which Angel is haunted by dreams of his past murders only to find that these crimes have been taking place in the real world. He believes that he may be returning to his old ways subconsciously and it is only in the second act that he realizes it is Penn, a protégé of Angelus from "back in the day," recently arrived in Los Angeles. Here we see a merging of the two types of flashback styles established by Whedon in the earlier *Buffy* episodes: the parallel of past and present events and the literal emergence of a person from Angel's past into his present—a trend that continued with the return of Darla in season two, Holtz in season three, Angelus and the Beast in season four, and Spike in season five.

The episode "Prodigal" was originally intended to focus on the character Detective Kate Lockley and her relationship with her father. Tim Minear, however, pitched the episode with a slightly different twist that would link it much closer with Angel's character arc established by Whedon in "Becoming" by suggesting that the story of Angel and his father should be connected with Kate's story (Bratton 2000). In this episode, Minear picks up where Whedon's flashback of Liam being "turned" by Darla left off as we see the birth of Angelus as he crawls out of his grave and then confronts and murders his father. These moments crystallize his identity as a vampire and contribute to the series' mythology, for the episode establishes the origins of his name when Angelus tells his father that his sister let him into the house because "she thought I was an angel returned to her." More significantly, Minear transforms the flashback structure established by Whedon in "Becoming" to suit the thematic concerns of *Angel*. In "Becoming" flashbacks to the "big moments" in Angel's past life are intercut with moments in the present that will set the course of both Buffy and Angel. Unlike most flashbacks on *Angel*, this episode suggests that these images of the past are from Angel/Angelus's point of view, as they are introduced with a voiceover from Angel/Angelus, explaining "there's moments in your life that make you. That set the course of who you're goin' to be. Sometimes they are little subtle moments. Sometimes they are not. I'll show you what I mean." In this episode we see the earlier events in Angel's life in order to position the contemporary events as a continuation of his path.

In "Prodigal," however, the flashbacks do not originate from any point of view but are juxtaposed with the contemporary events to make a thematic connection for the audience. In this case, Angel's ultimately destructive and disturbing relationship with his father, which results in Angelus committing patricide, is related to Kate's more conventional dysfunctional father-daughter issues, ending in his death. The juxtaposition of these different events drives home the theme, explained by Darla to Angelus after his father's murder, "what we once were, informs all that we have become." Both Angel and Kate must live with their perceived complicity in their fathers' deaths, all of which informs who they will become. This pattern is once again used in Jim Kouf's script for "Five by Five" in which Faith's descent into darkness is juxtaposed with flashbacks to Angelus right before and after he was cursed by gypsies with the return of his soul. While Darla's response to a post-ensouled Angelus is to reject him because "You're not like me! You're not like anything!" the juxtaposition of these events with the downfall of Faith suggests quite the opposite. The flashbacks serve to prepare the audience for Faith's breakdown at the end of the episode and her decision to take Angel's path to redemption in "Sanctuary." Similarly in "Quickening" (3:8, by David Greenwalt) and "Lullaby" (3:9, by Jeffrey Bell), the murder of Holtz's wife and children by Angelus and Darla is intercut with the birth of their own child and the return of Holtz to seek his revenge. In this manner, the Angel narrative that began with Joss Whedon in "Becoming Part 1" developed, through the contributions of the *Angel* writing team, into an epic narrative in which all of the events of Angel's life, past and present, interact to inform the man and the mission.

The true test of collective creativity, however, comes when there are changes within the creative group. *Angel* faced this test in its fourth season on the air. While the first three seasons saw *Angel* develop from an extension of *Buffy the Vampire Slayer* into an independent series created by a core group of writers led by Joss Whedon, David Greenwalt, and Tim Minear, season four saw a major shake-up within the production team. Following unsatisfactory contract negotiations with Fox Television, David Greenwalt left *Angel* to go to ABC. At the same time, Joss Whedon was focusing his attention on bringing Mutant Enemy's third television series, *Firefly,* to the air and to do so he took Tim Minear away from *Angel* to be executive producer of *Firefly.* In a few short months, *Angel* lost its core senior writing staff. Joss Whedon was still in charge, but with three television series to oversee and his attention particularly focused on launching *Firefly* he was not able to give the show the same level of attention he had previously. To replace Greenwalt, David Simpkin was hired to serve as showrunner but he left after three months, just as production was beginning, because of professional differences. Eventually Jeffrey Bell, who had been part of the *Angel* team since season two, was promoted to this position. Adding to these staff changes, Steven DeKnight was invited over from *Buffy the Vampire Slayer,* while David Fury served as a consulting producer on *Angel,* spending most of the season jostling back and forth between the two shows.

Despite these changes, season four actually serves as the culmination of the series' operative arc narrative, with its virtual abandonment of the episodic in favor of a sustained story line. This move toward the extended narrative had been gradually introduced in season three with mini-narratives that spanned two or more episodes such as Darla's pregnancy and birth (3:7/8/9) and the Prophecy/kidnaping Connor episodes (3:14/15/16/17). In season four, however, this extended narrative begins with Cordelia's return from her place as a higher being in "Slouching toward Bethlehem" (4:4) and ends with the destruction of Jasmine in "Peace Out" (4:21). One of the explanations for this move is of course that with fewer writers working on the series, more intense collaboration was needed than had been in previous seasons, as evidenced by the increased number of episodes with multiple writer credits (DeKnight, qtd. in Nazzaro 2003, 52). As a result of this extensive collaboration, the narrative became increasingly interlinked.

This epic season also serves as a culmination of the previous years as numerous character and narrative arcs were addressed. In this season we see the destruction of Wolfram & Hart, the return of Faith, and the conclusion to the Fred/Gunn/Wesley love triangle. After three and a half seasons in which the characters anticipate and prepare for the return of Angel's evil alter ego, Angelus, the team finally faces him. Most significant, in "Inside Out" (4:17) writer Steven DeKnight offers an entire reinterpretation of events throughout the show, such as Darla's pregnancy, Connor's birth, Cordelia's inheritance of the visions, and her transformation into a higher being, as having been orchestrated by one of the Powers That Be to serve her own selfish aims.

While season five would return to a few of these themes, most notably the return of Wolfram & Hart, what is significant is the manner in which season four interweaves all of these themes into its apocalyptic narrative and does so from within a period of creative shake-up within Mutant Enemy. That the show managed to not only maintain its memory but situate memory at the center of the seasonal narrative during this period is final evidence that the creativity of the series did not emerge from one artistic force but from the collective imagination of an evolving team of writers at Mutant Enemy. As Jane Espenson explains, "It all begins with Joss. But it doesn't end there" (2003, ix).

"Creeped out and Comforted at the Same Time"
The Generic Hybridity of *Angel*

> [Angel]'s good personified, he's evil
> personified, but he's also kind of funny.
> *David Boreanaz (qtd. in Persons 1999,
> 11)*

*A*ngel was conceived as a hybrid text constructed through the creative contribution of a collection of writers and designed to walk the line between the episodic structure of a TV series and the continual narrative of the serial. Each episode has its own story, generic references, and visual style, while also contributing to the series' broader narrative arcs and generic iconography. Graeme Turner points out that "it is pointless to insist on generic purity in relation to television programs. Television genres and programming formats are notoriously hybridised" as their episodic structure facilitates genre playfulness while TV producers "often change aspects of their programmes in response to audience feedback." The result of these adjustments can, Turner argues, be "a change in genre" (2001, 6). Jason Mittell further suggests that contemporary television series are increasingly constructed through some form of generic hybridity, a marker of their position as postmodern texts (2004, xii). *Angel*'s hybridity is therefore part of this intrinsically televisual approach to genre. Furthermore, Jane Feuer suggests that in the multichannel landscape of contemporary television, in which audiences regularly flick through channels, heightened "genre recognition skills" are required in order to grab audience attention (1992, 158). As such the visual iconography of a series is all the more important, and on *Angel* this involves evoking the show's multiple generic allusions through the series' distinctly cinematic visual style. In particular, the show's generic interplay conveys the complexity of Angel himself, for as a vampire he is equally a hybrid, marking the fusion of living and dead, human and demon. He is further hybridized as a vampire with a soul, a mixture of good and evil, while as a "champion" he is a combination of superhero and hard-boiled detective, romantic lead and comic buffoon. It is *Angel*'s hybrid use of genre and its visual style, described by David Bianculli as "[m]ore colorful and corporate, more flashy and glamorous; think *Miami Vice* after dark" (1999), that I would like to discuss in this chapter.

The series is most often described as film noir (see Abbott 2003; Jacob 2005; Sayer 2004; Stoy 2005) partly because of the decision to situate the show in Los Angeles, a city with a legacy of film noir associations. That a large proportion of the series was shot on location and—given the central protagonist is a vampire—at night made noir a logical genre and visual style around which to base the new series. As Benjamin Jacob explains, "evidence of *Angel*'s assimilation of film noir visual style can be found throughout the series: scenes are steeped in shadow; faces are half-lit, figures silhouetted; visual symbols of entrapment—images of barred windows, banisters and iron railings—abound; and motifs of the night and the city are continually interwoven" (2005, 80). This has led to a notable visual style for primetime television on a network most associated with teenage and family viewing. When programmed in its third season to follow the WB's successful family series *7th Heaven*, David Greenwalt described the decision as being "a little like following *Mary Poppins* with *Seven*," a comparison based as much on the series' visual style as its dark content (qtd. in Malcolm 2002, 58). As Rhonda V. Wilcox and David Lavery point out, "[n]ot since *The X-Files* has a series so consistently made beautiful use of darkness as the chiaroscuro of *Angel*" (2005, 225).

What is of interest is the manner in which this chiaroscuro is used to express not the nihilism of film noir, best expressed in such films as *Detour* (Edgar G. Ulmer, 1945) and *Kiss Me Deadly* (Robert Aldrich, 1955), but rather the moral ambiguity of the Angel universe. In the season two episode "Belonging" (2:20), Lorne explains to Angel what his home dimension Pylea is like.

> Lorne: Talk about screwed-up values. A world of only good and evil. Black and white. No gray. No music. No art. Just champions roaming the countryside fighting for justice. Boring! Got a problem, solve it with a sword. No one ever admits to having actual feelings, let alone talks about 'em. Can you imagine living in a place like that?
>
> Angel: Not really.

Here Lorne describes Pylea as black and white and Angel can't imagine such a place for his world, in contrast, is a world of gray. In season one Angel explains that he longs for the simplicity of evil for "there is no guilt. No torment. No consequences. It's pure. I remember what it was like—sometimes I miss that kind of clarity" ("Blind Date," 1:21). In season five, when faced with another questionable decision, Wesley points out that they are finding themselves yet again "in a bit of a gray area" ("Soul Purpose," 5:10). Yet the adoption of a film noir aesthetic means that visually there are no gray areas in *Angel*. Instead the ambiguity is expressed through darkness. One example occurs toward the end of "Blind Date" when Wesley informs Angel that while he may question the effectiveness of his mission when faced with the evil of Wolfram & Hart (W&H), "there is a design, Angel—hidden in the chaos as it may be but—it's there. And you have your place in it." While this gives Angel hope, the final shots of the episode capture the ambiguity of that fate through their use of darkness. As Lindsey McDonald (Christian Kane), Angel's nemesis in much of seasons one, two, and five, chooses to remain with W&H and embrace his position on the side of evil, he turns to look out his window at the nighttime cityscape beyond. The scene dissolves to a medium close-up of Angel overlooking a similar cityscape, surrounded by darkness with tiny pinpricks of light coming from the buildings in the distance. The camera slowly tracks around him and he appears to have a smile on his face, suggesting a sense of satisfaction with the knowledge that he is a part of a grand design. But as the tracking shot continues, the portion of his face that was previously in light slowly falls into darkness, leaving a very noirish image of Angel's divided self, one half of his face in light and the other consumed by darkness.

The implication of this sequence is that while Lindsey may have made his choice, Angel's future remains undecided. He may indeed figure within a grand scheme, but it is unclear as to whether it will be on the side of good or evil. Here the iconography of film noir, the contrast between light and dark, is used to establish Angel's hybridity and the ambiguity of his destiny.

Angel is not, however, singularly defined by its film noir visual style but rather draws on and interconnects a range of generic references to create a coherent hybrid form, a complex narrative, and a rich visual landscape for the series. It is in fact this generic hybridity that distinguishes it from other

A classic noir image in "Blind Date."

vampire television series such as *Dark Shadows* (ABC, 1966–71), *The Night Stalker* (ABC, 1972), *Kindred: The Embraced* (Fox Network, 1996), and *Forever Knight* (CBS, 1992–96). From week to week, *Angel* could change its generic formula, including episodes that primarily fall within genre parameters such as horror ("I've Got You under My Skin," "Billy," and "Hellbound"); film noir ("Are You Now or Have You Ever Been"); melodrama ("Lullaby," "Waiting in the Wings"); musical ("The House Always Wins"); comedy ("Guise Will Be Guise," "Spin the Bottle," "Smile Time"); and fantasy ("Over the Rainbow," "Through the Looking Glass," and "There's No Place Like Plrtz Glrb"). Each of these episodes has a self-contained narrative that uses genre as a tool for structuring the story and dictating the look of the episode.

One example of a stand-alone horror episode, conceived as such by the writers, Tim Minear and Jeffrey Bell, is "Billy" (3:6). The story focuses on the team's pursuit of a part-demon named Billy who can transform men into murderous misogynists. Even here, however, the conventions of horror are built on an investigative narrative as Wesley acquires police reports, Fred listens in on a police scanner, the team questions witnesses, and Wesley takes a blood sample from the crime scene to investigate. Horror becomes the structuring generic influence when the team realizes that Billy's bodily secretions are the source of an infection that causes those who come into physical contact with him to commit monstrous acts of physical and psychological violence against women. The episode contains brief but shocking sequences of violence, such as Cordelia's vision of a woman being stabbed by her husband, and W&H lawyer Gavin Park (Daniel Dae Kim) grabbing colleague Lilah Morgan (Stephanie Romonov) by her hair and throwing her into a glass cabinet before throttling her. In both cases, although the full extent of the attack is withheld, the horror is conveyed through the sudden intrusion of this violent outburst within a rather mundane conversation. Furthermore, both sequences use fast cutting and jarring camera movements to suggest the brutality of the moment.

Various stylistic techniques including composition, camera movement, and lighting are used to build suspense and horror as Angel's right-hand man, Wesley, now under Billy's demonic influence after examining a sample of the demon's blood, turns his increasingly violent attention to his colleague and friend, Winifred "Fred" Burkle. In the scene, Wesley begins to behave strangely as he questions Fred about Cordelia's whereabouts. Catching her in a lie, Wesley, his face framed in a low angle shot and partially in shadow, tells Fred, "[L]ie to me again—and we're going to have a problem." Here this unsettling framing, along with Alexis Denisof's uncharacteristically cold delivery of this statement, informs the audience that something is amiss. This is reaffirmed throughout the rest of the scene when Wesley is repeatedly framed in rather tight, claustrophobic, and shadowed compositions. These conventions, often associated with film noir, here create a more intense aura of danger as they are structured around the usually gentle character who, up until this point, has lacked the moral ambiguity usually associated with Angel. Another notable composition that repositions Wesley as a figure of horror occurs when he, pictured in close-up and making full use of widescreen composition, turns to look at the weapons cabinet behind him. This common feature within the *Angel* mise-en-scène is here reinterpreted along generic lines. What was once a signifier of the team's demon-fighting superhero status becomes transformed into objects of horror.

33

As Wesley begins to hunt for Fred, the episode fully embraces the conventions of the horror genre to create a gothic mise-en-scène through the use of expressionistic lighting, long empty corridors, and derelict and dilapidated rooms,

Mise-en-scène of horror in "Billy."

enhanced by the presence of an axe-toting Wesley stalking the corridors. Aware of the inevitable comparison to the horror classic *The Shining* (Stanley Kubrick, 1980), the staging of the sequence deliberately undermines this similarity (Minear and Bell 2003). Unlike Jack Nicholson, Denisof delivers a restrained performance, appearing calmly menacing and calculating in his deduction of Fred's whereabouts and articulate in his misogynist condemnation of the female sex. The otherworldly steadicam style for which *The Shining* was famous is replaced by a slow and methodical camera movement, following Wesley as he checks each room. The subtle and rather childlike musical accompaniment to this sequence further emphasizes its chilling quality.

Much like *Buffy the Vampire Slayer,* the episode also works along the lines of much postmodern horror as it knowingly subverts the classic conventions of the genre that present women as victims by having each of the women save themselves. More significant, while the episode is ambiguous about the nature of Billy's effect on men—for it is unclear whether his touch changed the men or brought out something within them—the implication is that it is Wesley who is victimized by Billy. His body is penetrated by Billy's blood (see chapter 3 for a discussion of the theme of bodily penetration within the horror genre) and he is transformed against his will from his usually gentle persona into a violent attacker. As a result, at the end of the episode it is Wesley who is traumatized by the preceding events as opposed to Fred. In fact, she tries to comfort Wesley by telling him, "[I]t wasn't something in you, Wesley. It was something that was *done to you*" (my emphasis). Here the use of horror not only offers an effective and dramatic stand-alone episode but actually works to shape Wesley's character development by influencing later narrative events in terms of his relationship with Fred and his gradual descent into darkness throughout seasons three and four when he is forced to leave Angel Investigations.

On top of this isolated use of genre, each season has an overarching theme that draws the episodes together under a particular generic umbrella. Season one is film noir/detective while season two introduces, Caritos, the demon-karaoke bar, in which the characters regularly express and explore their problems through song. Season three is a family melodrama built around the return of pregnant Darla, Angel's former vampire-lover, the birth of Angel and Darla's son, Connor (Vincent Kartheiser), and the breakdown of Angel's family at Angel Investigations. Season four falls within the conventions of the disaster film as the team must overcome the effects of a supernatural catastrophe, while season five uses the move to Wolfram & Hart's L.A. branch as a means to integrate the courtroom and office drama into the generic mix. What is significant here is that genres are not abandoned but integrated with the noir landscape on both a seasonal and episodic level to create *Angel*'s cinematic aesthetic through which the series' narrative and themes are expressed.

While "Billy" operates largely as a horror story, other episodes deliberately integrate the conventions of different genres to reinscribe them with added meaning. The episode "Lullaby" (3:9) operates as an example of family melodrama with its narrative focused on Darla's pregnancy, her anxieties over being a mother, and the birth of her and Angel's baby. That both Darla and Angel are vampires who should be incapable of creating life introduces elements of horror and apocalypse into the mix, for no one knows what the offspring of two vampires will be. These anxieties are, however, only an exaggerated version of the fears all parents face; no one knows what his or her child will become or what impact the child will make upon the world. As Wesley informs Lilah, "[E]very child born carries into the world the possibility of salvation or slaughter," to which Lilah responds, "And one born of two vampires carries it in spades" ("Tomorrow," 3:22). Furthermore, flashbacks to Angelus and Darla's murder of Holtz's family infuses the present with an epic significance for it intertwines the fears and anxieties associated with childbirth and parenthood, the traditional subject of melodrama, with Holtz's centuries-old quest for vengeance. Simultaneously, Holtz's attempt to murder Angel and Darla by blowing up Caritos, an act more in keeping with the action genre, is here reinscribed as melodrama.

That the episode consciously operates as melodrama is supported by its visual style. As Thomas Elsaessar explains, melodrama is characterized by "a sublimation of dramatic conflict into decor, colour, gesture, and composition of frame, which in the best melodramas is perfectly thematised in terms of the characters' emotional and psychological predicaments" (1987, 52). Two scenes that best illustrate this are Angel and Darla's rooftop discussion of the baby and the actual birthing scene. In the first sequence Darla and Angel meet on the roof of the Roslyn hotel overlooking downtown Los Angeles. The location serves to separate them from the rest of the world as they are elevated above the city, surrounded by a romantic blue fog, with the lights of the city in the distance. Here they are untouched by the reality of the world below as Darla, a soulless vampire, offers her first expression of maternal love for the child she is carrying. Amid the wonder of her newfound emotion is horror at the recognition that the love she is feeling is a result of the ensouled baby inside her. When he is born, she will once again become the soulless monster who can only offer her human baby "ugly death." As she struggles with her fate, her conflicted emotions are expressed in the blue light that surrounds the two vampires and is reflected on Darla's face as she cries for the love she will never remember feeling. This form of electric blue is in fact strongly associated with the notion of soulfulness and is used as an expression of repressed emotion throughout much of season two as it serves as a backdrop within Caritos, a space that encourages introspection and self-exploration. This thematic use of mise-en-scène is reiterated later in "Lullaby" as Angel confronts the possibility that his baby might die, and the depths of his emotions are expressed through the blue curtained backdrop that surrounds him and serves as an emotional echo to the earlier scene.[1]

The birth of the baby is deliberately contrasted with the rooftop scene, for Angel and Darla are no longer positioned to overlook the city but are instead collapsed on the ground within its labyrinthine back alleys. In the process of escaping from a burning Caritos, under attack from Holtz, Angel and Darla both confront the possibility that their baby might die and the realization that this might be justified given their murder of Holtz's wife and children. The family melodramas of these three characters are here intertwined. Holtz's obsession with and fury at the two vampires who destroyed all those he loved is conveyed as he walks through the bar in dramatic slow motion, surrounded by burning flames. In this intense action sequence, the theme of family is clearly articulated. In the alley, as Darla tells Angel that the child is the only good thing they ever did together and prepares herself for the sacrifice she must make, she is framed by Angel on the right and Fred on the left, both overcome with emotion. Here the excessive rain pouring down in torrents over the trio expresses the intense emotion of the sequence—a prophecy had declared that "the heavens [would] weep" and indeed they do. The flickering of the fire from Caritos as it is mirrored on Darla's face also captures the emotions surrounding their centuries-long relationship as she reflects on the horrible acts, including killing Angel in a similar alley and transforming him into a vampire, that brought her to this one good moment as she stakes herself to give birth to their baby. In these scenes "Lullaby" interweaves various

The heavens weep as Darla prepares to die in "Lullaby."

genre conventions into its melodramatic form as a means of intensifying and expanding this particular narrative strand.

In contrast, other episodes draw on a range of distinct generic references to make different narrative points or develop character.[2] In doing so, those references can be used to make certain narrative, character, or plot points explicit. "The Shroud of Rahmon" (2:8) is an episode that integrates conventions of film noir, heist narrative, horror, comedy, and buddy cop movie. The episode is told in film noir–style flashback and is based around the story of a heist gone wrong as an inter-species team of thieves, in which Angel and Gunn are operating undercover, steal an ancient shroud, infused with the evil spirit of the demon who was buried in it, that drives all those in its proximity mad. To reinforce its horror atmosphere, the episode guest stars horror actor Tony Todd, most renowned for his role in *Candyman* (Bernard Rose,

1992), as a violent and monstrous demon who elevates the potential danger within the narrative, while it also positions Angel and Gunn as antagonistic "buddy cop" partners. Here the normal tensions and competitiveness exhibited by these two experienced demon-hunters are made more violent by the presence of the shroud and establish certain hostilities and prejudices held by Gunn against Angel that will be developed and explored in "That Old Gang of Mine" (3:3). More significant, the fact that Angel is a vampire who must fight to control his inner demon makes the threat of the shroud and the risk attached to his involvement with it all the more horrific.

The integration of noir and horror conventions at the beginning of the episode addresses these implications for Angel's character arc. The episode begins after the main events of the narrative have taken place as the police question Wesley, a structure that is reminiscent of such noir classics as *Murder, My Sweet* (Edward Dmytryk, 1944) and *DOA* (Rudolph Maté, 1950). The sequence is knowingly shot in noir fashion. Wesley is positioned against a deep black background while the high key lighting, coming from a source directly over the table, creates a series of shadows around his face. Furthermore, the framing of the sequence involves very tight and claustrophobic close-ups from the front and side, while the police officers speak primarily from offscreen or the background of the frame. In this manner, Wesley's position is one of isolation. His narration, however, begins to integrate conventions of noir with horror for his comments and tone possess the pessimism of film noir and yet they also suggest a madness that belies the police's attempt to get rational answers to their questions. He speaks as if to himself in incomplete sentences and half-formed thoughts and behaves as if traumatized by horrific events that defy normal experience.

She shouldn't have been there. She didn't know. I had to warn him. He didn't know what he was getting into. None of them did. If they did—[Look of concern on his face.] You didn't bring it here did you? [Then relaxes and looks away with a smile.] No-no-no—then it would be too late for all of us. He grabbed her hard. Very hard. [Looks up at the police officers.] I'm quite good with the ladies myself you know. [Police: "Just tell us what happened."] It all went horribly wrong.

The sequence then dissolves to an image of horror as a woman's body is shown falling to the ground in slow motion, accompanied by the sound of an anguished cry, as the camera tracks past the body and into a close-up of Angel with blood on his lips. Here noir and horror merge into one. Wesley is remorseful for what has happened but also suggests that what went wrong was not the heist but rather placing Angel in this situation where he would be at risk of becoming evil again. He tells the police officer, "He should never have been there. Of all people he should never. You don't tell him what to do. He's the boss. He helps people you know—when he's not in trouble himself." Wesley's tone in this sequence is horrified and tinged with an air of tragic circumstance. The integration of two genres in this episode reinforces the precarious position that Angel holds in terms of helping others while also trying to control himself.

Finally, we must consider the significance of parody in any discussion of genre. Steve Neale and Frank Krutnik argue that "parodies work by drawing upon such [genre] conventions in order to make us laugh" (1990, 18). As a result the conventions of one genre become subordinate to the conventions of comedy. A film such as *Scary Movie* (Keenen Ivory Wayans, 2000) is generally considered a comedy rather then a horror film because it generates humor by playing on our familiarity with horror conventions. In television, however, Mittell argues that while "the host genre is usually mocked within parodies, it can still provide more conventional associations and pleasures" (2004, 160).[3] *Angel* successfully integrates parody within its generic matrix without sacrificing the integrity of the other genres. What it does achieve through this hybridity, however, is a reconsideration and redefinition of the conventions of genre.

Steve Parks noted after the broadcast of the show's first episode, "[W]ill it [*Angel*] satisfy *Buffy* fans? Not if *Angel* doesn't loosen up and take itself a bit less seriously" (1999, 3). This comment, however, does not recognize that even from the first episode the show was intent on loosening up as it sought to parody the representation of the hero, be that action, romantic, noir, or superhero. As Joss Whedon explains, what makes *Angel's* story an interesting one to tell is that he is a "big strong hero" who is "so incredibly messed up and [has] so many emotional problems" (Whedon 2001). For instance in "City Of" (1:1) Angel's lone hero image, well established on *Buffy*, is undercut by the revelation that he avoids social interaction not because he is deliberately mysterious but because he isn't good with people. This aspect of Angel's personality is comically brought home as he struggles to initiate a conversation with a waitress and by his rather bemused expression as a Hollywood agent gives him his card and tells him he's "a beautiful, beautiful man. Call me. This isn't a come on. I'm in a very serious relationship with a landscape architect." In a reverse of this scene, in "Lonely Hearts" (1:2) Angel's attempts to interact with the crowd in a busy nightclub are misinterpreted as Angel is shown assuring a rather tall and annoyed-looking man that "seriously, I wasn't hitting on you." Clearly Angel is out of his depth in the big city.

Furthermore, his position as the broody and Byronic hero, carefully constructed on *Buffy* in order to portray him as the ideal teenage romantic lead, is mercilessly mocked and parodied throughout the series. In particular, those around him regularly call attention to his overplayed sense of melancholy. In "She" (1:13) Angel attends Cordelia's house party, after which she sarcastically thanks him for coming by pointing out, "You know how parties are. You are always worried that no one is going to suck the energy out of the room like a giant black hole of boring despair but there you were in the clinch!" In "In the Dark" (1:3), Oz gently pokes fun at Angel's position as a detective hero when he asks Cordelia if Angel has a hat and gun, to which she responds, "Just fangs." The vampire Spike in the same episode offers a biting parody of Angel's position as a superhero when, while watching Angel and one of his clients from a safe distance, he delivers his own version of their conversation: "You see, I was once a bad-ass vampire but love and a pesky curse defanged me. And now I'm just a big fluffy puppy with bad teeth. . . . Helping those in need's my job and working up a load of sexual tension and prancing away like a magnificent poof is truly thanks enough. . . . Evil's still afoot and I'm almost out of that nancy-boy hair gel I like so much. Quickly to the Angelmobile—away." In this commentary, Spike evokes and mocks the image of Angel as a Batman-like superhero by describing Angel's car as the Angelmobile in the language of the camp 1960s *Batman* TV series (see Halfyard 2005 for a discussion of Angel and Batman). He also undermines Angel's virility as a hero by describing him as "defanged" by the curse and points out the effeminacy of his use of hair product. These are comic themes that return to haunt Angel throughout the series. They do not, however, undermine Angel's position as a hero, for he repeatedly performs heroic acts and makes personal sacrifices. What these comedy interventions do achieve is to undercut traditional representations of the superhero as strong, suave, and masculine in favor of a more human representation. Angel is physically strong but emotionally vulnerable; he is socially awkward and the entire notion of "masculinity" regularly comes under attack.

The differing approaches to genre adopted by the writers and directors on *Angel* exemplify the fluidity and permeability of genre within contemporary television. They further demonstrate the significance of genre hybridity to the series' narrative structure as well as its visual style. It is through our understanding of the iconography of genre that the complexity of its narrative is conveyed, requiring the audience to identify the generic shorthand in order to fully engage with character and narrative development. Furthermore, the show emphasizes the importance of its visual style by having the hybridity and ambiguity of *Angel*'s "world of gray" expressed visually through darkness tinged with a dazzling display of light and color.

"Does Giant Tentacle Spew Come out with Dry Cleaning?"
Angel and TV Horror

> Are you expecting any big vomiting here—because I saw the movie.
>
> *Cordelia to Angel as they prepare an exorcism. ("I've Got You under My Skin," 1:14)*

In the previous chapter I discussed the episode "Billy" (3:6) as an example of the horror genre. Many fans and horror academics would argue, however, that horror and television are contradictory terms. As Mark Jancovich and Nathan Hunt have pointed out, "[C]ertain sections of horror fandom see television horror as inherently inauthentic by virtue of its appearance on such a mainstream medium. . . . For these horror fans, television, the home of safe, sanitized programming, is opposed to 'real' horror—low budget, dangerous, and distinguished by its handling of taboo material" (2004, 33). By this argument the levels of censorship that are often a part of the television landscape, particularly on American networks in which the positioning of the TV in the home presupposes that its primary market is the family audience, place restrictions on any attempts to engage with horror in its "truest" form.

Furthermore, the commercial nature of network television also puts pressure on producers to ensure that TV material is suitable for a diverse audience and therefore appealing to potential advertisers. In contrast, the horror market is generally perceived as niche. As Matt Hills explains, the perception is that "in authentic horror [i.e., film and literature] anything goes . . . by contrast, TV horror is not 'really' horror precisely because it cannot go all-out to scare audiences: types of graphic 'splatter' horror that are possible in novels and films are generally less permissible in made-for-TV horror" (2005, 115). Although there are generally more restrictions imposed on TV horror than in contemporary film production, it is important to note that the genre existed in film long before the relaxation of censorship in 1968 with the formation of the Motion Picture Association of America, which many argue was a contributing factor to the evolution of the modern horror genre (Waller 1987a, 5–6). It is therefore inaccurate to suggest that the presence of censorship restrictions precludes television from producing horror. In fact, television has a long history of producing made-for-television horror films such as *Dracula* (CBS, 1973), *Trilogy of Terror* (ABC, 1975), and *Salem's Lot* (CBS, 1979), as well as long-running horror serials and anthology series including *Dark Shadows* (ABC, 1966–71), *American Gothic* (CBS, 1995–96), *Night Gallery* (NBC, 1970–73), *Tales from the Darkside* (Paramount Television, 1984–88), and *Friday the 13th: The Series* (Paramount Television, 1987–90). S. S. Prawer argues that TV horror movies like Dan Curtis's *The Night Stalker*[1] and its sequel, *The Night Strangler,* share much in common with "B" grade horror movies in terms of subject matter and production context as "they are made under similar restraints of money, location, and shooting-time" (1980, 20). Furthermore, Helen Wheatley's analysis of gothic television has demonstrated that the programming of a particular kind of horror material, most notably domestically set gothic tales of terror, in the home on television adds to the experience of horror (2006). Horror is, therefore, more than simply the explicit display of gore for, as Gregory Waller points out, "the made-for-television horror movie is the heir to Victorian ghost stories, Val Lewton's RKO productions in the 1940s, and classics of 'indirect' horror like *Dead of Night* (1946) and *The Haunting* (1963)" (1987b, 148).

The argument that TV horror is not "true" horror because it cannot be as graphic as its film equivalents also fails to address the fact that in recent years TV has increasingly been able to engage in more graphic depictions of horror than ever before. In fact, *Angel* sits at a pivotal moment in which American television, still in the midst of a major industrial transition as networks and channels continue to fragment and programming strategies change, was readdressing its relationship to horror, or more broadly its relationship to graphic displays of body horror. While *The X-Files* (Fox Network, 1993–2002) is often described as a hybrid of the forensic investigative drama and science fiction, episodes such as "Squeeze" (1:3), "Darkness Falls" (1:20), "Tooms" (1:21), and "Home" (4:2) offer self-contained horror stories, in terms of content, atmosphere, and graphic representation of the body. Their positioning within the narrative arc of the series, however, imbeds the horror genre within a complex web of generic hybridity that enables television critics to ignore the show's position as TV horror in favor of its science fiction credentials despite the fact that, as Catherine Johnson has pointed out, Chris Carter "claimed the original idea for *The X-Files* stemmed from a desire to redress the lack of horror in the primetime network television schedules" (2005, 101).[2] Recent series, however, like *Night Stalker* (ABC, 2005), *Supernatural* (CW, 2005–), *Masters of Horror* (Showtime, 2005–7), *Dexter* (Showtime, 2006–), and even the BBC series *Jekyll* (2007) have been unashamedly able to declare themselves as horror both in terms of advertising and through their overt embracing of horror conventions, demonstrating a changing attitude toward the genre as TV output becomes increasingly splintered across a vast array of channels and media outlets.

Before this recent renaissance of horror on television, the relaxation of censorship around images of body horror has been increasingly demonstrated in mainstream genres. In the 1990s, as argued by Jason Jacobs, new medical dramas like *ER* (NBC, 1994–) and *Chicago Hope* (CBS, 1994–2000) introduced "graphic depictions of serious injury" into primetime programming, leading to a new form of body spectacle. Jacobs explains, "For the audience, these dramas connected and nurtured a popular fascination with decay, death and the destruction of the body. They presented a 'morbid gaze'—the visualisation of the horrible but routine body trauma—within a context of procedural and ethical rules, and the professional language of science and medicine" (2003, 1). This "morbid gaze" was tempered, however, by the fact that these invasive procedures are done "to bring it [the body] back to health and life. . . . The meaning of such butchery that we see is firmly closed, directed to positive healing rather than violent destruction" (69). This is distinguished from the horror genre in which the spectacle of the wounded body, according to Jacobs, is treated as "a reward for suspense and fear" (69). Similarly, more recent forensic series, like *CSI: Crime Scene Investigation* (CBS, 2000–), offer equally transgressive and oftentimes shocking representations of the dead body, but in this case it is the fact that the corpse is treated as a stable object, present to serve as evidence for the solving of crime, that makes it acceptable. As Deborah Jermyn argues, however, there is a tension between the series' realist and scientific rationales and the spectacle that is offered up by its flashy aesthetics and its focus on the corpse and its "gross corporeality" (2007).

47

Angel is a series that while engaging in a creative inter-play of genre hybridity also uses its position as a vampire TV series to work quite openly within the horror genre. With a vampire as the lead character, the series is largely set at night, the prime temporal location for horror, and within an array of labyrinthine locations including sewers, tunnels, dark al-leys, and abandoned buildings. Furthermore, on a weekly basis Angel and his team confront a wide range of classic hor-ror monsters such as vengeful spirits ("Rm w/a Vu"), possess-ing demons ("I've Got You under My Skin," 1:14), zombies ("Habeas Corpses," 4:8), werewolves ("Unleashed," 5:3), and of course countless vampires. As a result of the embracing of the horror genre, unlike *ER* and *CSI*, the series faced greater restrictions in terms of what it could show in this context

(see Minear and Bell 2003). Yet by operating within horror conventions, it was able to openly address the indeterminacy and liminality of the human body. Elsewhere I have argued that "[t]he vampires in *Buffy* are, like the humans that sur-round them, singularly defined by their bodies. They burn, they feel pain, they can be sick, they can be poisoned" (2001). The emphasis on the materiality of the vampire body is a means of disembedding the vampire from traditional folklore, literature, and classic cinema such as *Nosferatu* (F. W. Murnau, 1922) and *Dracula* (Tod Browning, 1931), which represented the vampire as an ethereal and transformative creature of superstition. On *Buffy* vampires like Angel and Spike in particular are presented as all the more human, for although they cannot age or die, they are humanized through their physicality. On *Angel,* however, this materiality of both the vampire and human body takes on a different meaning. While the body in *ER* is something to be fixed or cured, and in *CSI* it is a "speaking witness" to crime, on *Angel* it is some-thing that is always under attack, redefining its boundaries or undergoing processes of transformation. In this chapter I would therefore like to analyze *Angel* as a horror text in a period of transition within television, still restricted from fully engaging in the graphic display associated with the genre but pushing the boundaries of what is acceptable within TV horror. At the same time the series challenges the modern perception of the body, as evidenced by more mainstream series where it is presented as stable, contained, and comprehensible. On *Angel*, the body may be tangible and penetrable, but it remains indecipherable.

Pushing the Boundaries of TV Horror

> I am going to have your skin peeled off and stapled back on inside out.
>
> *Lilah Morgan ("Quickening," 3:8)*

This threat is delivered by Lilah Morgan to a junior staffer when she is confronted by internal treachery at Wolfram & Hart. This line is a clear example of the series' preoccupation with the body in torment. While we never see Lilah act out this threat, the implication is clear: the risk of death is not sufficient to evoke terror in Lilah's staff, or the audience, but the anticipation of the painful mutilation of the body is far more effective. As Philip Brophy argues, one of the defining features of the contemporary horror film of the 1980s was "the destruction of the Body. The contemporary Horror film tends to play not so much on the broad fear of Death, but more precisely on the fear of one's own body, of how one controls and relates to it" (1986, 8). Recent horror franchises such as *Saw* and *Hostel*,[3] through their graphic displays of torture and bodily destruction, demonstrate that this emphasis on the body continues to be a key preoccupation of the genre. More specifically, Brophy argues that what is so disturbing about these films is how they convey "a graphic sense of physicality, accentuating the very real presence of the body on screen" (8). Even though we don't see it happen,

Lilah's choice of words, to *peel* off skin, *staple* it back on, *inside out*, were carefully selected as they present an evocative image of not only the "destruction of the body" but the precision with which it would be achieved. Here the writers achieve a "graphic sense of physicality" as well as articulating one of the fundamental premises of modern horror, the fear of the transgression and/or rupture of the boundaries and borders of the body.

The notion of the border is itself a key concept within any understanding of horror. The gothic genre in literature and film deliberately haunts the borders between living and dead, day and night, conscious and subconscious, civilization and barbarism, and present and past. Julia Kristeva, defining abject horror as a response to impurity, argues that that which does not "respect borders, positions, rules" but does "[disturb] identity, system, order" is impure (1982, 4). Barbara Creed particularly sees the modern horror film as an ideal space for an exploration of the abject for the genre is full of images of monsters that cross the border "between human and inhuman, man and beast . . . normal and the supernatural, good and evil" (1993, 11). Similarly, Noël Carroll argues that "many cases of impurity are generated by what . . . I called interstitial and categorical contradictoriness. Impurity involves a conflict between two or more standing cultural categories" (1990, 43). Here Carroll locates the horror within our cognitive understanding that the monster crosses the boundary between accepted physical, social, or cultural categories. What all of these approaches have in common is an understanding that horror emerges where borders are blurred. This theme permeates *Angel*.

The emphasis on the transgression of borders is achieved through language, as in the quote by Lilah, but also varying degrees of graphic display. In their discussion of *Angel* as TV horror, Matt Hills and Rebecca Williams argue that in response to the restrictions imposed on the series, *Angel* often engages with images of abject horror but through a restricted version of it: "Where *Angel* does depict the sliminess of abjection . . . it tends to use slime as a less objectionable stand-in for imagery that, it is implied, would be far more revolting" (2005, 207). According to Hills and Williams, the abject representation of the body does exist within the series but through implication or a less offensive substitute rather than overt representation. This strategy is utilized in "That Old Gang of Mine" (3:3) when Angel and his team discover that rather benign and peaceful demons are being targeted for murder. The first demon to die is the snitch Merle (Matthew James). After entering his lair, he is confronted by an intruder who remains offscreen. As Merle backs away in fear, the scene cuts to a shot of his shadow on the wall as the sound of a sword slicing the air is heard. The sequence then cuts very quickly between positive and negative footage of Merle's shadow as he struggles with his attacker, interrupted by one cutaway to a spray of green blood on the wall. The sound of the sword, the violence of the fast cutting, and the spray of blood all stand in for the violence taking place offscreen. This strategy does, therefore, effectively evoke the conventions of horror without alienating the network and the audience, and in this case also serves to conceal the identity of the murderers. In addition to this approach, however, the series also contains countless on-screen images of body horror.

In the first instance, the very nature of many of the demons or monsters faced by Angel Investigations overtly challenges or redefines bodily boundaries. For instance, in "Lonely Hearts" (1:2) Angel pursues a parasitic demon that literally burrows into a human body in order to possess it for a few days before having to find a new human host. The episode offers glimpses of the demon, in the shape of a phallic creature protruding from a vaginal opening in the host body, as it digs its way into the back of its next victim in a graphic display of penetration, leaving behind the desiccated and bloody body of its previous host. The episode "I Fall to Pieces" (1:4) has Angel confront a human doctor who has mastered the techniques of psychic surgery to such a degree that he is able to detach individual parts of his body and control them remotely so that he can be in more than one place at a time. In one scene he sits in his office and watches the woman who has become the object of his obsession through his eye that is hovering outside her window. Later, he stands outside her building as his hands creep into her apartment, climb into her bed, and crawl over her body. In "Epiphany" (2:16) Skilosh demons impregnate Cordelia as they inject their spawn into the back of her skull. While the actual moment of penetration is withheld from the camera, it is evocatively conveyed, in a scene reminiscent of the work of David Cronenberg, when Cordelia is held down as the leader of the clan stands behind her and a small bug-like creature crawls out of his mouth. That bodily boundaries have been broken is emphasized after the pseudo-rape scene as Cordelia reaches behind her head to find a large third eye protruding from her skull.

Furthermore, the series often features moments of bodily destruction or carnage in which the borders of the body are extended, penetrated, or destroyed. The episode "Parting Gifts" (1:10) raises a particularly interesting instance of bodily mutilation when a demon attempts to auction Cordelia's seer eyes to the highest bidder. The sale leads to an explicit discussion of the extracting of her eyes that was perceived to be too graphic for broadcast on Britain's Channel Four in the 6 P.M. programming slot. The entire discussion was cut.[4]

> Wolfram & Hart lawyer: We won't be needing the body. My employers have requested that the eyes be extracted.
> Benny: An extraction is a very delicate process. We run the risk of damaging the gift. It's gonna cost you—an extra thou.

W&H lawyer: Please—extraction is always included in
the price.

Benny: Not with seers' eyes.

W&H lawyer: Never heard of such a thing.

Benny: Never been such a thing like this on the market—an extra thousand or you take it as is.

W&H lawyer: Okay.

[Benny approaches Cordelia with an eye-gouging in-
strument, Cordy's eyes open wide in abject terror, and
the sequence fades to black.]

Cordelia's eyes are of course never gouged out but what is
significant here is the emphasis on the potential bodily dismemberment of the show's primary heroine. This scene ends
not on a threat to Cordelia's life but her eyes. Furthermore,
the horror of this threat is enhanced by the specificity of television as the moment is suspended until after the commercial break when Angel and Wesley arrive in time to save her.
Finally, this scene, like Lilah's threat in "Quickening,"
demonstrates that on *Angel* language can be as graphic and
transgressive as visual representation for here even the notion of gouging out Cordelia's eyes, discussed in a business-
like manner, was considered too much for late afternoon television.

In other episodes we are provided with more graphic depictions of bodily mutilation. In "She" (1:13) Cordelia's vision contains explicit images of a man's skin being burned
and his eyeball popping out toward the camera in close-up.
In "Underneath" (5:17) the vast physical prowess of Wolfram
& Hart's new liaison to the Senior Partners, Hamilton, is conveyed when he literally punches a security guard through the
chest, a close-up of his bloody hand protruding from the
body emphasizing the penetrative violence of his actions. In
these examples, the camera does not linger on these mo-

53

ments of horror in the way we would expect from a horror film. Instead the cutting is fast, opting for a shocking glimpse of body horror instead of a slow perusal of the graphic moment. It is the fact that we do not expect such moments on TV that makes them effective despite their brevity. In the context of prime-time television, when we don't expect to see graphic displays of body horror, the "glimpse" becomes all the more disturbing.

Other episodes, however, do provide a more lingering gaze on the gore, demonstrating that what is considered acceptable is changing. In "Birthday" (3:11) Cordelia is introduced to the ghost of Tammy, the last human to have carried the visions from the Powers That Be. The force of the visions was so strong that they eventually killed her, and as she explains this to Cordelia, she slowly turns to reveal that the back of her head is missing, leaving a bloody hole in her skull. The vividness of this moment presages the fifth season episode "Hellbound" (5:4), described by Hills and Williams as "one of *Angel*'s more horrific episodes," in which Spike is confronted by a series of ghosts haunting Wolfram & Hart, each featuring different images of bodily mutilation (2005, 212). One man chops his fingers off, another is burned, and another has a broken neck while one woman removes a large shard of glass protruding from her bloody eye in order to slice Spike across the face. Later in a séance, the clairvoyant is attacked by the spirit of a dark sorcerer also haunting the law firm, and as he invisibly squeezes the life out of her, her nose begins to bleed before she spews forth a spray of blood and collapses dead on the table.

Redefining the Boundaries of the Body

This focus on bodily torment is indicative of more than simply the desire to shock and repel the TV audience but rather

Body horror in "Hellbound."

connects to a central preoccupation of the horror genre itself. Barbara Creed argues that the genre's obsession "with the materiality of the body" "points to another, more complex concern—an obsession with the nature of the 'self.' Images of the dismembered, mutilated, disintegrating body suggest that the body is invested with fears and anxieties which are actually felt about the self. . . . The monstrous body of horror may appear to be only flesh, bones, and sinew, but I would argue that the destruction of the physical body is used as a metaphor to point to the possibility that the self is also transitional, fragile and fragmented" (1995, 143). This focus on the fragility of the self becomes apparent in its application to *Angel* when we consider the way in which the bodies of the series' main protagonists are repeatedly under threat of invasion, mutilation, and dismemberment. While the staff of Angel Investigations may regularly confront monsters that defy physical or cultural categories as well as the abject body (Cordelia, Wesley, Lorne, Fred, and Gunn are often shown cleaning up demon body parts or returning from a mission covered in demon blood), they also face the threat to the sanctity of their own body and identity. Each of the main characters undergoes some form of violent bodily attack that serves to explore anxieties about the nature of the "self" as it is reshaped and redefined.

In the first instance the characters are under threat of violating forces puncturing their way into the body, not only penetrating its outer boundaries but thrusting itself through to the character's very soul. This is quite literally what happens to Lorne when W&H drill into his skull to extract information ("Slouching toward Bethlehem," 4:4). Cordelia, however, undergoes a more sustained attack to her body beginning with her inheritance of the visions from the Powers That Be, for each vision of violence and monstrosity is thrust into her brain with such ferocity that she loses "control of [her] entire central nervous system," falling to the ground and convulsing ("Parting Gifts"). As Philip Brophy argues, "The horror is conveyed through torture and agony of havoc wrought upon a body devoid of control" (1986, 10). This becomes all the more apparent at the end of the first season of *Angel* when Cordelia is cursed to receive visions of all the horrors of the world at once, resulting in her descending into a schizophrenic seizure that can only be controlled through drug-induced catatonia ("To Shanshu in LA," 1:22). In "That Vision Thing" (3:2) this violation is made even more physical when Lilah hires a mystic to "hack into Cordelia's brain" and send her false visions. The visions break through into the real world by manifesting themselves on Cordelia's body in the form of severe claw marks across her abdomen, boils on her neck and arms, and finally extensive burns across her body. In "To Shanshu in LA," Cordelia's experience of the visions, while horrific and violent, do facilitate her transition into a stronger person as she comes to understand the importance of Angel's mission and the need to help the helpless. By "That Vision Thing," however, she begins to question her own strength to receive the visions and the Powers' rationale for doing this to her. Is it a punishment? What was once empowering becomes a reminder of her intense vulnerability.

Gunn is also the recipient of a similar psychic/physical invasion of his body when he agrees to have the knowledge of the law downloaded directly into his brain in season five. The penetration of his brain is conveyed in a reverse *CSI* shot, in which the camera appears to zoom out of a tunnel from the center of Gunn's brain to a long shot of a shirtless Gunn sitting in a doctor's chair, covered in wires and electrodes, breathless and bathed in sweat ("Conviction," 5:1). This violent insertion of knowledge into both Gunn and Cordelia, presented with an emphasis on the physicality of the invasion, initiates a process of transformation from within. While it initially provides both characters with a sense of purpose and the tools to do good, it also places them on the path to evil and an increasing alienation from their sense of self. Gunn is transformed into a form of cyborg, for this artificial insemination of the knowledge precipitates a change to his body and identity through technological intervention. This leads Gunn to compromise his ethics, and in so doing his identity, in order to maintain his new position, which inadvertently results in Fred's death. Cordelia's transformation is less visible but far more destructive, for accepting the visions and the various changes to her body demanded by the Powers, including becoming part demon, sets her on a path to complete invasion when she is physically and psychically taken over by one of the Powers That Be in season four.

Bodies on *Angel* are also presented and described as vessels to be cut open, emptied, or hollowed out. For instance, as punishment for his contribution to Fred's death, Gunn takes Lindsey's place in a Wolfram & Hart holding dimension in which he is tortured and has his heart cut out of his body everyday. While we never see this happen in detail, in "Origin" (5:18) we do get one graphic glimpse of the results of Gunn's ordeal when the torturer is shown dropping his heart into a basket filled with human hearts. After he walks away, Gunn's dead and bloody body is revealed lying sprawled on a table. The sequence cuts to a medium close-up of his chest cavity, cut open and empty save for copious amounts of blood. As the camera moves into close-up, the gaping hole in his chest begins to stitch itself back together.

While the first violation of Gunn, achieved through modern technology, served to compromise Gunn's identity, this experience, harking back to medieval torture, facilitates Gunn's gradual recuperation of the "self" as he is reminded, through the painful and daily penetration of his body, of his humanity. Yet even here there remains a form of alienating intervention as his body is made to mystically restore itself in order to repeat the process.

In the case of the possession of Fred's body by the god Illyria, the series enters into a much more ambiguous exploration of identity. First described as an infection by an unknown pathogen, destroying Fred's body from within, the doctors inform Angel that "her organs are *cooking*—in a day's

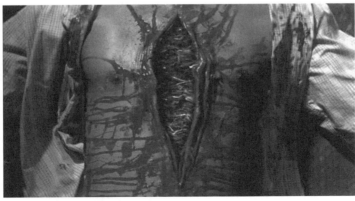

Gunn's invaded body in "Origin."

time they'll *liquefy*." Later Wesley explains that it is a more than an infection: "Fred's skin is *hardening* like a shell. I think she is being *hollowed out* so this thing can use her to gestate— *claw* its way back into the world." These passages describe an intensely physical and horrific attack on the body. Even Fred's spiritual demise is conveyed physically when Dr. Sparrow explains that her soul "was *consumed* by the fires of resurrection" ("Shells," 5:16). While we do not see what is happening to Fred from the inside, this violation of her body, as described by Angel and Wesley, in which she is hollowed out to facilitate the rebirth of another being, is a classic convention of such modern horror films as *Invasion of the Body Snatchers* (Philip Kaufman, 1978), *The Thing* (John Carpenter, 1982), and *The Fly* (David Cronenberg, 1986). As happens in these films, Fred's transformation brings about a serious consideration of the nature of the self when Angel and his team are confronted by a being who looks like Fred but is not her—or is it? Intermingled with Illyria's consciousness are Fred's memories and attachments to both place and people. Also, Illyria's consciousness has effectively been downloaded into Fred's body and, as Bronwen Calvert argues, it is through being embodied (i.e., existing in and through Fred's body) that Illyria comes to "metamorphose into Fred" (2007). In this manner Illyria is Fred or partially Fred. Through the birth of Illyria, we witness Fred's fusion with another being at a physical and spiritual level, and in this fusion she becomes all the more powerful and unruly for hers becomes a body that defies traditional rules, restraints, and boundaries.[5] Illyria cannot be held within her grave; her life force cannot be contained within her human body, nearly causing her to explode; she defies the restrictions of temporality by slowing down, speeding up, and traveling through time. She even breaks natural laws of anatomy by transforming herself back into Fred, telling Wesley, "It's a simple modulation of my form. I appear as I *choose*" ("The Girl in Question," 5:20). As Jennifer A. Hudson argues, "Since Illyria 'consumes' Fred's soul (and perhaps vice versa) besides taking her body, the energies of both constituents end up shifting in the subspace of the shell. Thus, Illyria's mystical rebirth transforms Fred's shell into a choric site of contradictions and absences where rigid boundaries between Illyria and Fred dissolve" (2005). This attack on Fred's body represents a challenge to the seeming permanency of identity and places Fred/Illyria within a liminal space; she is even more of a hybrid than any other character on the show as she is a mix of Fred and Illyria, dead and alive, human and God, male and female, and good and evil. Fred/Illyria blurs all boundaries of identity and moral certainty.

All of this leads us to Angel and Spike, both of whom undermine physical and cognitive boundaries. As vampires they are both living and dead and, according to the mythology of the Buffy/Angelverse, vampires contain two faces (human and demon) that can morph back and forth in a fluid transformation. Furthermore, Angel and Spike are vampires with souls, blurring the boundary between good and evil. They are both. The act of drinking blood is also a penetrative act that transgresses the boundaries of the body. While Angel gave up drinking human blood with the return of his soul, numerous episodes including "The Shroud of Rahmon" (2:8), "Power Play" (5:21), and "Not Fade Away" (5:22) show Angel biting into a human neck to drink, reinforced by the sounds of skin being penetrated and liquid being swallowed. Also, as pointed out by Hills and Williams, Spike's position as a ghost and vampire at the beginning of season five of *Angel* places him within a particularly transgressive and liminal space because he is doubly dead (2005, 211).

More significant is the representation of Angel's body. While the bodies of his colleagues undergo a form of attack by being cut open, penetrated, and/or hollowed out, Angel experiences all of these attacks to his being. In the 110 episodes of the series, Angel and Angelus are repeatedly stabbed ("War Zone," "Judgment," "Untouched," "Reprise"), staked ("Somnambulist," "The Ring," "Tomorrow," "Destiny"), shot ("Five by Five," "A New World," "Shiny Happy People"), beaten ("The Ring," "The Trial"), tortured ("In the Dark"), burned ("I've Got You Under My Skin," "The Trial"), hanged ("Are You Now or Have You Ever Been"), possessed ("Birthday," "Waiting in the Wings"), and body-swapped ("Carpe Noctum"). In "Soul Purpose" (5:10) he dreams of his chest cavity being surgically opened up and emptied while in "Ground State" (4:2) his heart is brought to life by the electrically charged super-thief Gwen, presented through a *CSI*-style shot of the electric charge racing through his system and jump-starting his heart. In "I Will Remember You" (1:8) he is transformed into a human by absorbing regenerative demon blood into his system, while in "Smile Time" (5:14) he is turned into a puppet. Furthermore, unlike other hybrid heroes or action figures like Blade, the Terminator, or even the ever-resistant Jack Bauer from TV's *24* (Fox Network, 2001–), Angel is not unaffected by these attacks but rather demonstrates the physical effect of this penetration. He is often presented as in pain, weak and unsteady on his feet, requiring the assistance of his colleagues to keep him going. As such the series simultaneously emphasizes the physical frailty of the human body while, through Angel's immortality, demonstrating the uncanniness of a body able to absorb and transcend these attacks to his being. Angel's position as a hero is therefore both challenged by the level of his suffering and reinforced by his ability to withstand it.[6] Elsewhere I have argued that contemporary vampire films like *Blade* (Stephen Norrington, 1988), *Underworld* (Len Wiseman, 2003), *Van Helsing* (Stephen Sommers, 2004), and *Underworld: Evolution* (Len Wiseman, 2006) have reinterpreted the vampire myth through the language of science and technology, and as a result the vampire body has increasingly been represented as defying its boundaries, "able to transcend and redefine them at their will" (2007). While *Angel* resists the lure of scientific explanation through genetics or hematology, preferring to maintain the supernatural rationale for vampirism, it shares with these films their preoccupation with challenging our understanding of the body. But while Blade's body is presented as a technological cyborg, Angel's body remains a mystery.

As I've demonstrated, the body on *Angel* is constantly under attack or undergoing processes of transformation. As a result, the show embodies the central preoccupations of the contemporary horror genre and gives expression, as argued by Andrew Tudor, to "people's experience of social fragmentation and to the constantly threatening confrontation between embattled 'selves' and the risky and unreliable world that they inhabit" (1995, 40). By situating this cultural fascination with the body at the heart of its episodic and serial narrative as well as its representation of its hero, *Angel* demonstrates the same tendency toward transgression and taboo breaking that typically characterizes the horror film. While restrictions on the presentation of horror may apply within television, unlike its big screen counterpart, the *Angel* creators developed and employed innovative strategies that remind us that TV horror exists and flourishes within the modern television landscape.

"Cavemen vs. Astronauts— Weapons to Be Determined"
Angel, Masculinity, and Male Friendship

> At least I've got company. You and Me— together again. Like Hope and Crosby— Stills and Nash—Chico and the Man.
> *Spike to Angel ("Hellbound," 5:4)*

In developing *Angel* as a stand-alone series, David Greenwalt comments that in many ways it was a tougher show to create than *Buffy* "because the metaphor isn't so simple; but ultimately, we've finally figured out that *Buffy* is about how hard it is to be a woman and *Angel* is about how hard it is to be a man" (qtd. in Nazzaro 2002, 158). This approach to the new series is not entirely surprising. Lorna Jowett argues that "it follows that in trying to destabilize traditional representation of femininity, especially through role reversal, *Buffy* must offer a concomitant alternative version of masculinity," which, she argues, it does (2005, 119). It therefore makes sense that the producers would proceed from the success of its post-feminist series and approach the male-focused show with a similar intention. More significantly, *Angel,* like *Buffy,* came at a time when issues surrounding gender were being contested and debated across academia,

63

the media, and popular culture. Notions of gender as constructed and performative, previously applied to discussions of femininity, were increasingly being used to address changing conceptions of masculinity (Butler 1990; Berger, Wallis, and Watson 1995). Furthermore, the concept of "masculinity in crisis," often perceived as originating within the 1960s civil rights and feminist movements and compounded by changing social and economic factors in which white masculinity is seen to be displaced by an increasingly multicultural society, gained cultural currency in the 1990s as exemplified by films such as *Falling Down* (Joel Schumacher, 1993), *Disclosure* (Barry Levinson, 1994), and *Fight Club* (David Fincher, 1999) (Faludi 2000; Robinson 2000). These cultural preoccupations are made manifest in *Angel*'s male characters, Angel, Wesley, Gunn, Lorne, Spike, and Connor, each of whom embodies very different notions of masculinity that change or are put into crisis throughout the series—as Wesley tells Fred, "I don't know what kind of man I am anymore" ("Billy," 3:6).[1] Furthermore, Angel's changing relationship to the other men in the series, from his father-son relationship with Connor to his familial bond with Wesley, offers an insightful consideration of the fluid nature of masculinity, challenging the belief that masculinity is fixed and instead replacing it with "an idea of multiple masculinities in which rigid boundaries of sexual and gender representation are blurred and even redrawn" (Berger, Wallis, and Watson 1995, 3). In this chapter I will specifically examine the privileging of male friendship through the evocation of the buddy genre, as exemplified by Angel's relationships with Doyle and later Spike, as a means of considering how *Angel* sits within these cultural debates about masculinity and homosocial behavior.[2]

Lynn C. Spangler's analysis of "male friendship in prime-time television" demonstrates that there is a longstanding tradition of male relationships on TV, from the western series of the 1950s and 1960s to the detective series of the 1970s and 1980s, but in these shows the nature of the relationships between men is largely defined by action, not emotion. Men may bond in these series but "emotional disclosure is not necessarily a part of their relationships" (1992, 105). Such early situational comedies like *The Honeymooners* (CBS, 1955–56) that did focus on a male friendship defined not by action but by shared experience, intimacy, and personal problems were eventually replaced by the family situation comedy in which the source of emotional bonding is located within the nuclear family (*Father Knows Best,* CBS/NBC, 1954–60; *Leave It to Beaver,* CBS/ABC, 1957–63). Another exception to this tradition of male friendship is *Star Trek* (NBC, 1966–69), a series that dealt quite overtly with the friendship between Captain Kirk and First Officer Spock. But even though many of its episodes are founded on the emotional bond between the characters, unrestrained outbursts of emotion are usually treated with humor. As Spock is so proud of his lack, or restraint, of human emotions, his occasional outbursts (as in "Amok Time" when he realizes that Kirk is still alive) are met with condescending laughter on the part of Kirk and Bones, who revel in Spock's lack of control—his humanness, which Spock sees as weakness. In this manner *Star Trek* tries to have it both ways. It valorizes emotion but also constrains it. While the 1980s saw a rise, according to Spangler, of more "sensitive men in both comedy and drama," most of the men were "happily married with their wives as their best friends" or Vietnam veterans, whose friendship is depicted as an unspoken bond "developed during the Vietnam war" (e.g., *Magnum P.I.,* CBS, 1980–88). According to Spangler, "men able to discuss intimate subjects with each other were found mostly in programmes such as *thirtysomething* (ABC, 1987–91), targeted at more upscale, educated men and women" (108–9). A notable exception was the buddy cop series *Starsky and Hutch* (ABC, 1975–79), in which the friendship between the two police officers is a driving force within the narrative and where occasional episodes, such as "Shoot-Out" (1:14) and "A Coffin for Starsky" (1:21), specifically focus on the intense bond between the partners and feature the men openly expressing their feelings to each other.[3] All of these programs, however, fit in to what Susan Jeffords describes as the transition to the New Man, characterized by "increasingly emotive displays of masculine sensitivities, traumas, and burdens" (1993, 259). Looking at the action genre, Jeffords notes that "externality and spectacle have begun to give way to a presumably more internalized masculine dimension. . . . Recent Hollywood male star/heroes have been constructed as more internalized versions of their historical counterparts. More film time is devoted to explorations of their ethical dilemmas, emotional traumas, and less to their skill with weapons, their athletic abilities, or their gutsy showdowns of opponents" (245). Responding to these notions of the "new man" prevalent within Western society, the creators of *Angel* offer, however, an action series in which emotional bonding and expression go hand in hand with the action.

When he first appears on his series, Angel is the embodiment of what Milette Shamir and Jennifer Travis describe as one of the most "well-entrenched truisms about masculinity: that it connotes total control of emotion, that it mandates emotional inexpressivity, that it entraps in emotional isolation, that boys, in short, don't cry" (2002, 1). Angel chooses isolation; he is a man of few words; and, given the nature of his predicament, being a vampire with a soul—not to mention the nasty loophole to his curse that says that a moment of perfect happiness will result in the loss of his soul—he must control all emotions and desires. Restraint and self-denial are his defining characteristics. He is, in many ways, the cliché of white masculinity. The character of Francis Doyle, however, seeks to challenge this image of masculinity. Brought in by the Powers That Be to set Angel on his path, it is Doyle who establishes the mission for Angel, the hero and the series, when he explains that the task at hand is about more than fighting. It is not enough to fight evil and destroy the monsters, Doyle tells Angel. It is really about "reaching out to people, showing them that there is love and hope still left in this world. . . . It is about letting them in your heart. It is not just saving lives, it's saving souls. Hey—possibly your own in the process" ("City Of," 1:1). This mission statement is therefore about more than helping the helpless; it is about rethinking the nature of heroism and masculinity.

Once placing Angel on his path, Doyle is presented in the first nine episodes of the series very much as the sidekick to Angel's hero, even described as such by Buffy ("I Will Remember You," 1:8). Doyle's initial role is effectively to provide Angel with information (through his visions) and access to the seedy underworld of Los Angeles. His position as sidekick is emphasized by that fact that there is something shady about Doyle when compared to Angel's silent nobility. He gambles, owes money, and drinks too much. Furthermore, he does not demonstrate Angel's bravery or personal commitment to action. When Angel gets ready to take on the vampire "corporate" tycoon Russell Winters in "City Of," Doyle wishes Angel luck, saying he will be there with him in spirit. Angel, however, informs Doyle that he is driving, to which Doyle offers a panicked response: "No. No. I'm not combat ready, man—I'm just the messenger." Angel's retort, "And I'm the message," sums up the role of hero and sidekick. Even when Doyle does attempt a moment of heroism, trying to drive through the fortress-like gates when he hears shots coming from inside Winters's mansion, the scene is played with humor as the car bounces off the gates, to which Doyle responds, "Good gate." In this first episode of the series, the formula is therefore established. Angel is the hero, Doyle is his connection to the Powers, and, as Doyle points out, Cordelia provides Angel's "connection to the world. She has a very humanizing influence."

The subsequent episodes, however, undermine this easy formula and clear-cut distinction between characters. What increasingly becomes apparent is that Doyle is himself the humanizing influence that will enable Angel to make a connection to the world. While the three characters are often depicted as working and fighting alongside each other, or more often Angel does the fighting and Cordelia and Doyle do the cleanup, throughout these episodes, Angel and Doyle are equally depicted conversing and sharing their problems. In "Lonely Hearts" (1:2) it begins simply by Doyle urging Angel to go out and have some fun (partly as a means for Doyle himself to be able to go out with Cordelia). By episode three ("In the Dark," 1:3), however, Doyle's desire to relieve some of Angel's self-imposed suffering takes on a greater significance when Oz, crossing over from *Buffy*, arrives from Sunnydale to give Angel the Gem of Amara, a talisman that will render a vampire impervious to harm. While Angel regards this gift cautiously, Doyle sees this as Angel's salvation. This episode ends with the first of a series of heart-to-heart conversations that take place between Angel and Doyle as Angel, having worn the ring for the day, enjoys his final sunset. In this conversation, Doyle is horrified to realize that Angel plans to destroy the ring, and the two men discuss Angel's need for redemption and his reasons for not opting for the "quick fix." Angel's argument that daytime people have help while nighttime people need him shows his own commitment to the mission that Doyle gave him in the first episode. This is a scene of sharing between men. Doyle is genuinely concerned about Angel but is also personally unsettled by the selflessness of Angel's heroic nature. This scene marks Doyle's first step on his own path of redemption where he will move from sidekick to hero. It is notable that the sequence is shot as they watch a sunset together—traditionally a romantic moment, one that Angel has never been able to share with Buffy but does share with Doyle. The romance of the sequence is of course safely undercut by humor as Angel admits to Doyle at the end of the scene that he was about to crack under torture.

This conversation is followed by numerous similar moments of sharing in the next few episodes in which the two men help and guide each other through their personal problems, as well as learn about each other's strengths and weaknesses. In "Rm w/a Vu" (1:5) Angel recognizes that Doyle is in trouble (this time from loan sharks and bounty hunters) and offers to help. When the bounty hunter demon asks Angel why a vampire would help a demon half-breed, Angel doesn't answer but the implication is that it is because they are friends. In "Bachelor Party" (1:7), when Doyle's wife, Harriet, shows up looking for a divorce so she can remarry, Doyle is thrown into an emotional turmoil and only Angel can help him by playing both the hero and the friend. Angel agrees to follow Harriet's fiancé to prove that there is something wrong with him, but when he is revealed to be an honest and peace-loving demon (or so we are meant to think), Angel helps Doyle realize that he must let go of Harriet in order to move on. Finally, in the episode "Hero" (1:9), Angel opens up to Doyle about his becoming human in the previous episode, "I Will Remember You," and his brief time with Buffy before choosing to turn back time and be a champion again.

> Doyle: Human! You were a real, live, flesh and blood human being—and you and Buffy?? You had the one thing you wanted in your unnaturally long life and you gave it back?!
>
> Angel: Maybe I was wrong.
>
> Doyle: Or maybe Cordelia was right—about you being the real deal in the hero department. See, I would have chosen the pleasures of the flesh over duty and honor any day of the week. I just don't have that strength.

Angel: You never know your strength until you're tested.

Doyle: Come on—you've lived and loved and lost and fought and vanquished inside a day, and I'm still trying to work up the nerve to ask Cordy out for dinner.

This sequence is significant on a number of fronts. It shows Angel opening up about himself and his doubts about his decisions in the way that he encourages Doyle to do. It once again raises the significance of redemption and the necessary sacrifices that are required to find it. And it demonstrates that through their friendship Angel is learning to be more human while Doyle is learning to be a hero. This theme culminates at the end of the episode when roles are reversed and it is revealed that the hero of the episode's title is Doyle and not Angel. Here we get the final personal exchange between the two men. As Angel prepares to sacrifice himself to save a clan of peaceful half-demons, he looks to Doyle to understand his decision and to say good-bye. This is a very tender silent moment between the two men, with Cordelia in the background.

Doyle, of course, does understand what is needed and, in his own act of friendship and heroism, knocks Angel out and makes the sacrifice himself. Through this final act, Doyle not only saves the day but teaches Angel his final lesson about humanity: "sometimes it isn't about saving lives but saving souls"—in this case, Doyle's. Angel must accept the loss of his friend, whom he finally refers to as such in "Parting Gifts" (1:10). As Angel explains to Cordelia in "I've Got You under My Skin" (1:14), having spent centuries surrounded by death, this is the first time Angel has had to suffer through the death of a loved one and the absence felt through the loss of a friend.

This emphasis on the intensity of the friendship between Angel and Doyle is indicative of a form of homosocial desire,

A tender farewell in "Hero."

which Eve Sedgwick argues exists on an "unbroken continuum" with homosexuality. The visibility of this continuum, she argues, is however disrupted by an "obligatory heterosexuality" (1985, 1, 3). To embrace male friendship is to overtly denounce homosexuality. This is generally achieved in two ways, first by overtly pronouncing the men's heterosexuality (through the presence of wives, girlfriends, love interests) and second through humor to disrupt any form of homosexual panic. On *Angel* both techniques are used. Angel of course is in many ways defined by his love for Buffy, particularly in the first season when his presence in L.A. is still presented as a result of their breakup. Doyle of course is presented with an ex-wife and a potential relationship with Cordelia. The subject of many of Angel and Doyle's discussions is their relationships or potential relationships with women. Having said this, the one relationship that they possess that is successful and satisfying is their friendship, while their romantic relationships are either futile or largely unrequited.

Furthermore, while humor is used in "In the Dark," as previously discussed, as a means of undercutting the romance of the sunset and the openness of the discussion, humor is also used to overtly acknowledge this continuum between homosocial desire and homosexuality rather than simply negate it. In "I Fall to Pieces" (1:4), Doyle explains to Cordelia why Angel is uncomfortable asking for money.

> Doyle: He likes playing the hero. Walking off into the dark, his long coat flowing behind him in that mysterious and attractive way.
> Cordy: Is this a private moment 'cause I could leave you alone.
> Doyle: I'm not saying I'm attracted to him. I'm just saying he projects a certain image.

Later as Angel walks away, shot from Doyle's point of view in slow motion as his coat flows behind him, Doyle admits, "Maybe I'm a little attracted." Here humor is used as a means of acknowledging the transgressive implications of their friendship while simultaneously rendering it safe. On *Angel*, however, the consistent use of humor serves primarily to call attention to transgression rather than undermine it. Here the "hero" shot of Angel with his coat flowing behind him, which is used quite seriously in the opening episode, "City Of," and is an iconic image featured weekly in the series' opening credits, is shown to be a potential sexual fetish. The use of humor here is less a way of getting around the sexual tension than a means of acknowledging it.

Humor as a transgressive mode of expression becomes far more significant in season five of *Angel* with the introduction of Spike into the series, a decision made for obvious commercial reasons as the networks hoped that Spike's popularity on *Buffy* would boost *Angel's* audience. While his presence didn't save the show from cancellation, it did provide the writing team with a golden opportunity to explore a relationship that had heretofore only been alluded to through various flashbacks and a brief overlap of the two characters on *Buffy* during which they were largely positioned as either enemies or rivals. Spike's arrival at Wolfram & Hart at the end of "Conviction" (5:1) repositions their relationship. They are no longer enemies but rather reluctant partners, made all the more complicated by their mutual affection for Buffy and their now shared position as vampires with souls. James Marsters sums up the comic antagonism between the two vampires: "I hope I'll make life as miserable as possible for Angel. I just absolutely want to be pitted against him; to have to work with him and hate him anyway is absolutely hilarious" (qtd. in Gross 2003b, 57). To work with and hate a partner is a fundamental characteristic of the buddy genre and much of the humor that surrounds the two characters when together is drawn from the series' use of these conventions in their enactment of the Spike-Angel relationship.

73

The buddy film is a genre that focuses on the often comic friendship between two men. The genre dates back to the classic team comedies of Laurel and Hardy, Abbott and Costello, and Hope and Crosby but truly matured in the 1970s with such films as *Butch Cassidy and the Sundance Kid* (George Roy Hill, 1969), *Easy Rider* (Dennis Hopper, 1969), and *Midnight Cowboy* (John Schlesinger, 1969). The rise of the buddy film in this period has been seen by critics from Molly Haskell to Robin Wood as a backlash from the feminist movement by creating male-centered narratives in which women were unnecessary. This serves as an example of the cultural response to what Sally Robinson describes as the perceived "decentring of white masculinity" in response to the civil rights and feminist movements (2000, 4). In the 1980s and 1990s, the buddy cop film took over from the buddy road movie and primarily addressed issues of racial otherness (*Lethal Weapon*, Richard Donner, 1987; *Die Hard*, John McTiernan, 1988), again with white masculinity positioned as traumatized or victimized, and which must be recouped through the action and buddy cop narrative. According to Robin Wood, the modern buddy film is usually characterized by a journey (or, in the case of a buddy cop film, an investigation), the marginalization of women, the absence of home, and what he describes as "the male love story," the placement of the film's emotional center within the male-male relationship (1986, 227–28). According to Cynthia Fuchs, "these films struggle to recognize 'homosocial behaviour' while keeping homosexual tensions below the surface" (1993, 196).

Micheline Klagsbrun Frank further argues that a large number of buddy films are characterized by the fact that the two men are fundamentally different or opposed in nature and are bound or trapped together as they undertake a life- or character-changing journey, which can be literal and/or spiritual. Frank argues that "the change has two dimensions: the formation of a bond or affiliation between the men and the individual overcoming of prejudice that involves reclaiming parts of the self" (1990, 123).

The introduction of Spike into *Angel* situates the two vampires within the context of the buddy film. There are numerous moments during season five that overtly acknowledge this generic heritage in their relationship. In "Just Rewards" (5:2), when Spike and Angel arrive at a necromancer's house and ask to be announced, Spike describes himself as Angel's "date." In "A Hole in the World" (5:15), when Angel finally admits that Spike is effectively driving him crazy and they can't go on like this, Spike asks, "Does this mean that we have to start annoying other people?" And of course the episode "The Girl in Question" (5:20) is an all-out buddy genre episode as it follows Angel and Spike on their escapades in Italy as they attempt to reconnect with Buffy.

While Doyle was clearly positioned as a sidekick because of his role as a supporting agent for the hero, Spike enters into the narrative as a hero of, arguably, equal measure to Angel—he has, as he constantly reminds Angel, just died to save the world ("Chosen," B7:22). Furthermore, he is also, like Angel, a vampire with a soul. While all of the main characters on the series contribute to the mission, up until this point no one had been in a position to challenge Angel's uniqueness as a champion. With the introduction of Spike, that uniqueness is removed much to Angel's annoyance. Spike's role as shadow to Angel, as discussed by Roz Kaveney, becomes all the more pronounced in season five as he literally becomes a shadow presence haunting Angel at Wolfram & Hart and later, when re-corporealized and released from his magical ties to the law firm, Spike literally becomes Angel as he takes on Angel's role as protector of nighttime Los Angeles (2004a, 10).

While the series makes great efforts to draw attention to their similarities, the show also emphasizes their different or opposite natures. Their opposition is neatly summed up in the scene from "A Hole in the World" that begins with Spike and Angel in the middle of a heated, and seemingly significant, argument only to be revealed that they were debating about who would win in a fight: cavemen or astronauts. This sequence demonstrates the humorous antagonism between the two men that is a key characteristic of the buddy film. The usually calm and restrained nature of Angel is thrown into a spin by the presence of Spike as they engage in this ridiculously overheated schoolyard debate. Angel's agitated movements and fast-talking delivery of his lines contrast with the stillness of Wesley when he enters the discussion. Here Wesley takes on the role usually attributed to Angel as the calm mediator; this scene is reminiscent of a similar scene in "The Ring" (1:16) in which Wesley and Cordelia engage in rather inane argument about Wesley's social life, or lack thereof, only to be chastised by Angel's silent and disapproving presence.

Another key characteristic of the buddy film that is utilized in this scene is the two-shot. Joss Whedon uses one take to cover the entire scene up until Wesley enters the room and the sequence cuts to his reaction. On the DVD commentary, Whedon comments on the significance of this approach to the comic scene: "Here is where I learned the two-shot lesson: if I just keep the camera going and don't give in to coverage, these two just, they come up so hard on each other—I think David has never been funnier than he is at the end of this shot" (2005b). The two-shot enables the actors to nuance their relationship and bring out the best in each other comically. It is not only the fact that they are in the same frame that makes this scene funny, but the manner in which the handheld camera follows the two actors from medium long shots linked together by a swish pan into a very tight head and shoulder shot as their hostility and frustration with each other build to a comic climax with Angel's childish outburst: "It's not about what I want!" Here we move from Spike's comic broad gestures and statements to an intense intimacy as the two men face each other down.

The cut to Wesley is deliberately designed to disrupt this tension and feel like an embarrassing intrusion on their intimacy. The two-shot is used regularly throughout the final season to situate Angel and Spike as comic antagonists. These shots not only play to the comic strengths of the actors but also provide visual reminders of their position as buddies—they are a functional dysfunctional heroic team.

Returning to the "cavemen vs. astronauts" scene, the most important element of the sequence in terms of their role as buddies is of course the content of the debate. According to Whedon, the debate originated when Doug Petrie from the

Angel and Spike face off in "A Hole in the World."

Buffy team came to the *Angel*-writers' room and wrote "Cavemen vs. Astronauts—weapons to be determined, who would win?" on the writers' board. This resulted in an extended and divisive argument within the writing team (Whedon 2005b). While the inclusion of the debate in the episode is a nod to the writers, it also serves as an eloquent summation of the fundamental differences between Angel and Spike—differences that continue to haunt them throughout this season. Spike argues that cavemen's primal, savage, brutal animal instinct gives them the advantage (all characteristics that easily define Spike's persona) while Angel espouses the importance of human evolution and teamwork. Angel of course has evolved through the course of the series from the lone crusader to a team player and leader who finds his strength in family.

Spike is the caveman to Angel's astronaut, but what is the significance of this opposition beyond offering periodic comic interludes? In her analysis of the odd-couple movie, Frank argues that "the premise of initial opposition . . . is based on the splitting off of unwanted attributes that are then objectified in the partner" (1990, 125). By this account, what they loathe in each other is what they want to deny in themselves. Angel resents Spike's free-spirited nature that enabled him to bounce back from re-ensoulment with little suffering—a couple of weeks crazy in a basement compared to Angel's century worth of suffering. Spike is the monster that Angel rejects in himself. For Spike, his comment that humans have evolved "into a bunch of namby-pamby self-analyzing wankers"—definitely a phrase he would use to describe Angel—confirms that he resents Angel's internal struggle with his past, which implicates Spike with his own past. Spike rejects the need to look inwardly.

Furthermore, what they want to deny in each other is that which they have in common, namely their past. Throughout the series Angel has been represented as a man who is haunted by his past, which every once and a while emerges into the present to torment him—Darla, Drusilla, Angelus, and Holtz. In this case, he is tormented by Spike, the most significant male vampire that has played a role in his life and yet until this season, the nature of their vampiric relationship was left unaddressed. In season five, however, we are reminded that their relationship as buddies began in their more uninhibited life as marauding vampires. In the episode "Destiny" (5:8) we are given a flashback of their first meeting in which the freshly vamped William/Spike is clearly drawn to Angelus's intensity. Angelus initiates William to the group by grabbing his hand and pushing it into the sunlight, forcing it to burn, as he asks, "Do you have any idea what it is like to have nothing but women as travel companions— night in and night out?" When Spike pulls his hand away, Angelus places his own hand into the light as he explains, "Don't mistake me. I do love the ladies but lately I've been wondering what it would be like to share the slaughter of innocence with another man. Don't think that makes me some kind of a deviant—do you?" This scene bears quite overt connotations of homosexuality through homosocial bonding driven home when Spike mimics Angel by placing his own hand into the light, which some might argue, as with many buddy films, is what Spike and Angel are seeking to reject or deny in themselves. The series, however, does not deny this homosexual tension but embraces the subtext we have come to expect of the buddy genre by overplaying it in scenes like this that remind us that Spike and Angel's status as vampires already makes them sexually and liminally transgressive (see Amy-Chinn 2005; Hills and Williams 2005) and is reinforced by Spike when he points out to Illyria that "Angel and me have never been intimate—except that once" ("Power Play," 5:21). They are vampires after all. That the series overtly acknowledges the homosocial/homosexual continuum that is kept beneath the surface of the buddy film is further demonstrated in "Destiny" as Angel and Spike race to find the cup of Eternal Torment, a competition that ends with a knockdown, drag-out fight, itself a convention of the buddy genre used to channel all of the unacknowledged sexual tension through an acceptable masculine outlet, but here made transgressive when the fight literally climaxes with Spike stabbing Angel in the shoulder with a wooden stake, a moment that is consciously replete with sexual and phallic symbolism.

Significantly, what the flashbacks in "Destiny" do represent to the vampires is their life as monsters—that which they have denied as vampires with souls. When looking at each other and their pasts they can only see the atrocities they have committed to their victims and to each other—as Spike tells Angel, "Drusilla sired me. You made me a monster." This shared past, however, increasingly shifts throughout the season from something to be denied and rejected to something that binds the vampires together that only they can understand as they continue on their journey to redemption. In "Damage" (5:11) and "Why We Fight" (5:13), both

Spike and Angel are haunted by the past—Spike by the psychotic Slayer Dana, who mistakes him for the man who tortured her as a child, and Angel by the only person he turned into a vampire after regaining his soul. Each of these episodes features a sequence in which the vampires must consider the implications of their past on their present search for salvation and it is up to the other to come and offer if not comfort then understanding. Like the earlier sequences with Doyle, these are intense moments of male sharing. Furthermore, in their discussion in "Damage" in which they explain what they were drawn to as vampires we see a more reflective version of the cavemen vs. astronauts discussion. For Spike it was the rush and the crunch of the fight while Angel was in it only for the evil. Here they acknowledge their own differences but also recognize that fundamentally they are the same—monsters who were once innocents. Similarly, the naval officer-turned-vampire who returns in "Why We Fight" searching for a "reason" echoes Spike and Angel's own search for a reason for all they have been through as humans, vampires with and without souls—a reason to keep fighting.

In these scenes we begin to see the results of the life- or character-changing journey that is so fundamental to the buddy film and, as Frank argues, the beginning of a "bond or affiliation between the men" and the gradual "overcoming of prejudice that involves reclaiming parts of the self" (1990, 123). This full transformation of Spike and Angel from odd-couple bickering and snapping at each other into a heroic buddy team takes place in "A Hole in the World," the episode that first shows Angel and Spike arguing semantics as Angel walks through the room with a sword through his chest (and of course also features the cavemen vs. astronauts debate) but ends with them united as heroes to save Fred. In this episode we once again see the use of the two-shot, this time from a low angle, to frame Angel and Spike as they leave their offices as Angel tells Spike, "Come on—let's save the day." This time it is used to emphasize their heroism, strength, and unity as opposed to their comic opposition. Later when they arrive at their destination and are attacked by guardians of the Deeper Well, a form of graveyard for the Old Gods, the sequence offers a comic wink at the conventional homosexual subtext of the buddy genre when Angel asks Spike to hold his hand and, surprisingly, Spike complies with little but a bemused look.

As Spike realizes that Angel holds garrote wire in his hand and responds with a knowing look, "St. Petersburg?" we are reminded of their history together, not only as heroic vampires with souls but, in this instance, their history as marauding vampires with a hundred years' worth of brawls and battles behind them. They use this history in order to work as a team. They embrace their past as vampires (with all of the sexual and physical liminality that that brings) in order to be champions.

Before we think that this journey is all about reinforcing notions of heroism and traditional masculinity as they fight

Angel and Spike stand together in "A Hole in the World."

to save the girl, we must remember that in this episode our heroes are unable to save Fred or, more to the point, they choose not to save her because the price to humanity is too high. The climax of their journey is, therefore, not the rescue of Fred but rather Angel's moment of realization that he can't sacrifice the world for her and Spike's silent understanding as he looks down at the Deeper Well and quietly remarks, "This goes all the way through—to the other side. So I figure there is a bloke somewhere around New Zealand, standing on a bridge like this one—looking back down at us. All the way down. There's a hole in the world. Seems like we ought to have known." Again a moment of sharing, reflection, and understanding between men takes priority over fighting and vanquishing monsters. Of course, Angel and Spike's relationship continues up until the final episode ("Not Fade Away," 5:22)—when Spike heartily volunteers to betray Angel—to be one of heroic opposition. Their strength is shown throughout this season to be in their similarities, in their differences, and in their friendship.

"It's a Little Outside the Box"
How *Angel* Breaks the Rules

We're turning this place inside out.
Angel ("Conviction," 5:1)

As the previous chapters have demonstrated, *Angel* exists as a distinct example of contemporary genre television, offering complex and ambitious narrative arcs and an exciting interplay of genre conventions, but it also stands as a site of unusual experimentation with the televisual form. Mere Smith points out that for the show's producers, Joss Whedon and David Greenwalt, "story is what matters . . . the story is everything" (2003), but evidence within the series demonstrates that an intrinsic element of the show was its readiness to break with convention and experiment at both a narrative and aesthetic level.[1] There are numerous episodes throughout the series that contribute to the narrative arc but also provide an outlet for outstanding creative experimentation. To conclude this examination of *Angel*, I intend to focus on three episodes—"Are You Now or Have You Ever Been?" (2:2), "Spin the Bottle" (4:6), and "Smile Time" (5:14)—that demonstrate how *Angel* regularly broke the conventions of television drama, stylistically, narratively, and generically, and challenged the audience to step outside the "box."

"Are You Now or Have You Ever Been," written by Tim Minear and directed by David Semel, was the first episode that attempted to break with the broader narrative arcs established in season one by offering a stand-alone mystery enveloped in nostalgia for classic Hollywood cinema. Opening on a photograph of an abandoned hotel—the Hyperion—the episode begins with Angel tasking Wesley and Cordelia with investigating its history. Right from this beginning the narrative stands out as anomalous to the series because the members of the team are not working for a particular client nor have they been sent a vision from the Powers That Be. Instead they are serving Angel's seemingly cryptic purpose. The episode then follows Angel and his team as they investigate the hotel and its dark history of crime, violence, and murder. Through a series of flashbacks, it is revealed that a post-ensoulment Angel, no longer feeding off humanity but not engaging with it either, lived at the hotel in 1952, where he encountered a young woman, Judy, who was hiding from the authorities, having stolen money from her employers. Overcome with fear and paranoia about being caught, she turns to Angel for help and support. Realizing that Judy's paranoia, along with that of others in the hotel, is being stoked by a demon who feeds off their fear, Angel decides to intervene. Before he can help, the residents of the hotel, led by Judy, who is now completely consumed by her paranoia, turn on him and lynch him in the hotel lobby. As a vampire, he does not die but leaves the hotel, but not before the demon reveals itself to Angel, taunting him about the fact that Angel's desire to help Judy had made her betrayal all the more satisfying and pointing out that there was a hotel full of people who needed his help. Angel tells the demon to "take 'em all" and leaves without turning back. The contemporary Angel has returned to the hotel to make up for past mistakes and complete the job he began in the 1950s by destroying the demon.

In so doing, he releases Judy who, completely absorbed by her guilt and remorse for her betrayal of Angel, has been kept alive by the demon for fifty years.

The episode establishes its main preoccupations by first situating the series within a broader cinematic heritage through allusions to classic Hollywood of the 1950s and then linking Angel's story to the culture of fear that existed beneath much of Hollywood in this period. The entire visual style of the flashbacks, including filtered lighting, slow and deliberate camera movements, and Hermannesque-style musical score, is designed to look and sound like an old Hollywood movie. This decidedly cinematic photographic style wraps Angel's story in nostalgia while conveying the haunting presence of the past. Furthermore, by locating the flashbacks in 1950s Hollywood, Minear was able to immerse his story within the conventions of film noir, a genre recognized for its embodiment of postwar cynicism. The episode also includes references to key films from the 1950s that are recognized as exemplifying the cultural climate of the period. Angel wears a red jacket much like James Dean in *Rebel with a Cause* (Nicholas Ray, 1955), an iconic exploration of social exclusion and emotional isolation. This association is reinforced when Angel's second meeting with Judy takes place at the Griffith's Observatory also featured in *Rebel*. Judy tells Angel she is from Salina, Kansas, the home of Kim Novak's Judy in *Vertigo* (Alfred Hitchcock, 1958)—while the contexts are different, both Judys are punished for masquerading as someone they are not. After being thrown out of the hotel by Angel, a private investigator returns sporting a bandage over his nose like Jack Nicholson in *Chinatown* (Roman Polanski, 1974), a film about the corruption of postwar Los Angeles. Finally, the focus on racial discrimination through Judy's story of "passing" as white, only to be fired and later jilted by her boyfriend when her secret is revealed, is reminiscent of Sarah Jane's story in *Imitation of Life* (Douglas Sirk, 1959).

These allusions position Angel's story within Hollywood tradition as well as signal the prevalent social and cultural concerns of the period, namely social exclusion, fear, paranoia, and betrayal. These themes are enhanced by situating the narrative in the context of the Hollywood Communist witch hunts and the House Un-American Activities Committee (HUAC) Senate hearings. One of the residents of the hotel is actually a blacklisted writer.[2] The hearings are played on the television in the background of numerous scenes in the hotel lobby as well as featuring as headlines in various newspapers throughout the episode. This very specific moment in American history lends the story context for its tale of paranoia and suspicion.

It is, however, the episode's non-linear structure and the manner in which the story moves seamlessly between the two periods—1952 and 2000—that overtly makes the episode distinct from others within the series. Although it is a flashback episode, it is quite different from the previous season's "Somnambulist" (1:11), "Prodigal" (1:15), and "Five by Five" (1:18) where, as explained by Minear, "you will have an A-plot in the present day and [unrelated] scenes in the past that reflect on the A-plot" (2002). In this case, the narrative is one story that begins in 1952 and ends in the present. Furthermore, traditionally, flashbacks are signposted in order to delineate past from present. On *Angel* this is generally achieved by a subtitle at the start of each flashback that situates location and time, such as "Romania 1898." In "Are You Now," however, the past and present are fused together through a series of fluid camera movements that establish a link between the periods. For instance, in the pre-credit sequence, after Angel leaves Wesley and Cordelia to get on with their assignment, the camera cuts to an extreme close-up of the black-and-white photograph of the Hyperion. The camera begins to track forward and as it pushes into the picture, the image transforms from a still photograph to a moving one as it turns from black and white to color and the cars in the frame begin to move. This image then dissolves to a close-up of the entrance of the hotel as a bellhop opens the door and, nodding toward the camera, invites us—the camera and the audience—in. Instead of simply presenting us with an image of the past to contrast with the present, we are being invited *into* the past. No subtitles explaining the location and time of the flashback are used. Instead the transition from present to past is conveyed by the use of slow motion and the period is simply evoked through the mise-en-scène—most significantly, the art direction of the hotel and the costumes of the actors. The audience is therefore expected to observe these surroundings and draw from them the narrative information they require.

This emphasis on observation is conveyed through the use of a roving camera that often circulates around the hotel as though it is an independent spirit. One such shot takes place near the beginning of the episode when present-day Angel explores the abandoned hotel. As he walks through the lobby, the sequence cuts to a shot of him from behind as he slowly walks to the right, out of frame, as the camera turns to the left and moves past a television airing the HUAC hearings. In this shot we have moved from the present to the past. The camera pans around the group watching the television, follows a man as he walks away from the TV, and then turns back toward screen right as another man chases a woman out of the lobby. As she exits the hotel, Angel—now in period costume—enters. While initially the camera seems to be instigated by Angel's point of view, this sequence demonstrates the camera's independence of Angel and suggests that the camera operates as a distinct character within the mise-en-scène, standing in for the demon that is haunting the hotel, fostering suspicion and paranoia in all the residents. In one flashback, the camera tracks past a group of hotel residents in the lobby, gossiping about a recent suicide, to rest on a close-up of an old man in the foreground of the frame as a voice whispers, "Are you sure you're safe here?"

More specifically, the camera movements, sometimes linked to Angel and sometimes not, suggest that both Angel and the demon are haunting the hotel in the past and the present. This is conveyed in the sequence after a hotel resident, staying in the room next to Angel, shoots himself. The shot of Angel quietly sipping a glass of blood, barely flinching at the sound of a gunshot next door, cuts to black and the next scene begins in black as the camera tracks from behind a wall, past the contemporary Angel walking up a corridor of the hotel, around the corner and into the 1950s as the hotel manager and bellhop come to investigate the suicide. Once inside the room, the two hotel employees discuss what to do about the body. Suddenly there is a small and unattributed track to the left as the sound of whispering is heard. As if responding to the sound, the manager follows the camera and steps into close-up: "Three in three months. They'll shut you down," the demon tells him. "Yes, they will," he responds. While the previous camera movement in the corridor was associated with Angel, this one is clearly linked to the demon, both quietly surveying and haunting the hotel.

The use of camera movement to convey the feeling of surveillance and paranoia is reaffirmed through the repeated use of slow and deliberate tracking shots along the corridor where Angel and Judy's rooms are located. In these scenes, such as the pre-credit sequence when the bellhop approaches Angel's room with trepidation or later as Angel walks along the corridor, detached and quietly observing those around him, the length of the corridor is extended by the slow camera movements and time is drawn out as the sequence repeatedly cuts from the bellhop or Angel's point of view to an objective shot of them as they slowly walk forward. These sequences, reminiscent of Jimmy Stewart's surveillance of Kim Novak in *Vertigo* in which shots of the observer and the observed are repeatedly intercut, use a seamless tracking camera to link each of the shots together in a fluid motion and create the impression that the characters are as much looked at as looking. It is important to remember that in *Vertigo,* while Jimmy Stewart's Scottie believes himself to be clandestinely observing Madeline/Novak, the audience spends as much time watching him as he does her and Madeline/Novak is also completely aware of his presence, performing for his gaze. These sequences in "Are You Now" create much the same effect of dual surveillance and as a result create an atmosphere of oppression and claustrophobia along the corridor.

This atmosphere takes concrete form later in the episode when Angel finds the residents of the hotel, their paranoia achieving climatic pitch, surrounding Judy and accusing her of being a liar and a murderer. This sequence intercuts shots of Angel slowly walking up the corridor, dropping his bag, and preparing to rescue Judy—and as such moving from watching to action—with shots of Judy surrounded by the mob, shouting and pulling at her. As she looks up at Angel, she steps forward, points at him, and yells, "It was him! Look in his room. Go ahead, look. He's got blood. He's a monster," and with this act betrays his friendship. This corridor that at first simply gave the impression of being oppressive becomes the location of real oppression as the mob gathers around Angel and knocks him to the ground before he passes out.

Judy's act of betrayal to protect herself, the group's decision to make Angel the scapegoat for all of their fears by lynching him in the hotel lobby, and Angel's choice to abandon Judy and the rest of the hotel residents to the caprice of the demon captures the paranoia and culture of self-preservation that defined the HUAC hearings and the period in general. As the demon tells Angel, "They feed me the worst and I kinda feed it right back to them. And the fear and prejudice turns to certainty and hate."

Suspicion and paranoia turn to violence in "Are You Now or Have You Ever Been."

In this episode, therefore, Minear and Semel experiment with the representation of space and time, fusing past and present, and draw on a more cinematic visual style and inter-textual heritage in order to situate Angel's simple story of a demon haunting a hotel within a broader context of para-noia, racism, and social intolerance. As such "Are You Now or Have You Ever Been" invites the audience into an alterna-tive universe that exists as a narrative and stylistic homage to the classic and dark days of Old Hollywood. Through these associations, however, the episode also contributes to the *Angel* narrative by exploring a dark moment in Angel's past when he had the opportunity to engage with humanity but instead gave in to his own fear and hate by turning his back on them. The episode seemingly shows the audience how far Angel has come since these events, but it also establishes the themes of prejudice, paranoia, and hate that will come to dominate the second season as Angel's battle with Wolfram & Hart becomes obsessive and all-consuming.

Joss Whedon's "Spin the Bottle" offers a very different

form of experimentation that is more preoccupied with drawing the audience out of the narrative by calling attention to its construction and in so doing inviting the audience to consider the processes of storytelling on an episodic and seasonal level. In trying to restore Cordelia's memory, lost since she returned from a period as a higher being, everyone in the team loses their adult memories when a magic spell backfires and they each end up thinking they are seventeen years old again. Waking up and finding themselves in an abandoned hotel with a group of strangers that includes a green-skinned, red-horned demon, the group quickly realizes that something is amiss and must investigate how and why they have been brought together. This story also provides us with a comic glimpse into what these characters would have been like as teenagers—Fred is a conspiracy geek looking to "score some weed"; Wesley is well intentioned but pompous and inept in his attempts to take charge of the group; Cordelia returns to her prima donna persona established on *Buffy*; Gunn is once again the streetwise, vampire-hunting teenager we first met in season one; and Angel is out of his depth, having returned to his seventeenth-century identity, Liam, who thinks the music coming from a small stereo is being played by "tiny minstrels" and that cars are shiny demons. The episode provides a comic respite from the developing apocalyptic atmosphere as well as the emotional fragmentation of the team that began at the end of season three and continues throughout season four. The previous season of *Buffy* had featured a similar story in which Willow inadvertently causes the entire Scooby Gang to lose their memory ("Tabula Rasa," B6:8). Both episodes use the memory spell to serve a similar purpose, which is to briefly restore our now seasoned and troubled demon-hunters to a state of innocence and wonder. "Spin the Bottle" in particular uses this narrative device to comically lampoon the generic conventions of the series as when the usually heroic Angel discovers that he is a vampire and is suddenly terrified that the others will discover his secret and kill him, or when Wesley—now a rather brooding demon-hunter—attempts to play the hero, resulting in his tumbling down the stairs in a spectacular pratfall. What makes this episode stand out as an experiment with narrative and storytelling conventions, however, is its use of a wraparound narration in which Lorne recounts the events of the episode as part of a cabaret performance.

This narration begins in the pre-credit sequence, which opens with Lorne, in silhouette against a bright red backdrop, singing, appropriately enough, "Memories." The lights slowly go up and Lorne is engulfed in a blue spotlight as he completes his song. The use of color in this sequence, the intense blue spotlight against the red backdrop, highlights the artificiality of the "performance," which is reinforced when the sequence cuts to a medium long shot revealing the microphone stand and piano behind him, with the smoke from a cigarette billowing up to add to the atmosphere. This color scheme is maintained throughout the episode, standing in stark contrast to the more natural mise-en-scène of the main story. Elaborate and colorful performing spaces were of course well established on *Angel* beginning in season two with the introduction of Caritos—Lorne's demon-karaoke bar—as well as in the Las Vegas–set episode "The House Always Wins" (4:3), which features a spectacular musical number. "Spin the Bottle" clearly emerges from this tradition within the series and yet the heavily stylized mise-en-scène, accompanied by a preference for close-up rather than the more theatrical long shots, seems to set the cabaret sequences both inside and outside the narrative diegesis. Andy Hallett, in full demon makeup, is clearly performing in character as Lorne and yet as narrator he is also positioned outside the story, looking on and commenting on events as they happen.

This is reinforced by the fact that the time and location of this cabaret performance are never clearly articulated.

Lorne's somber tone and air of doom, standing in stark contrast to the comedic tone of the episode's narrative, suggest that the performance is taking place after the rather apocalyptic events of season four and yet the narrative arc for the season provides no logical space for such a moment to take place. Furthermore, while the sounds of the audience are occasionally heard from offscreen, the audience is withheld from the scene, unlike the staging of the performances in Caritos and the Vegas episode that emphasize their presence. As a result, in "Spin the Bottle" Lorne's performance is directed at the camera and therefore at the television audience. This is particularly apparent when the pretext of the cabaret performance is briefly abandoned and Lorne interjects himself within the story but continues to speak to the camera and comment on the events occurring around him—at one point even going so far as to turn to the camera and acknowledge, "I know I'm still unconscious during this part of the story, but can you believe these mooks?" referring to the ridiculous antics of Wesley and Gunn. In this manner, the episode breaks the diegesis of the fictional world, and in so doing the conventions of most TV drama, by directly addressing the audience outside. The most overt instance of this occurs after one of the commercial breaks when the episode fades in to the stage as Lorne enters frame left and comments, "Well, those were some exciting products. Am I right? . . . Let's all think about buying some of those"—directly referring to the previous commercials and as such recognizing the show's place within a broader televisual flow. Furthermore, the progression of the story is regularly interrupted to allow Lorne space to comment, as when the shot of Lorne spinning across the room, after having been hit by Angel, is paused on-screen, so that the narrating Lorne can interject a slightly resentful, "Ow!"

These interruptions not only enable Lorne to comment on the events depicted on-screen but also direct their presentation. In the pre-credit sequence, after completing his song, Lorne begins his narration with the line, "Let me tell you a story. It starts with a kid," which initiates a swish pan to a medium shot of Angel's son, Connor, walking aggressively along a sidewalk, accompanied by a rock music score. The image of Connor turning toward the camera with an angry sneer on his face, however, suddenly freezes as Lorne interrupts and says, "No, actually, it really starts here," followed by a cut to a medium close-up of Cordelia asking Angel, "Were we in love?" Lorne's interruption deliberately calls attention to this transition in which the rock score is abruptly replaced by quiet romantic music, and the fast pace of Connor is replaced by the stillness of Cordelia and Angel. Similarly, as Lorne begins to explain the reasons for the tension and hostility building up between Wesley, Gunn, and Fred, his narration dictates the movements of the camera. For instance, as he describes how Fred had tried to kill her evil "professor by opening a portal" and how "Gunn didn't know that Wesley had helped her," the camera tracks in very quickly to a medium close-up of Wesley, followed by a swish pan to Gunn as Lorne continues, "Wesley didn't know that Gunn had killed the guy himself to save Fred from becoming a killer." The sequence concludes with a cut to a medium close-up of Fred as Lorne explains, "And Fred didn't know that Gunn"—camera pans left to Gunn—"was right then figuring out that Wesley"—camera pans left to Wesley—"had helped her try." In this sequence, the relationship between these three characters, as well as their thought processes as they piece together recent events, are conveyed through the moving camera as directed by Lorne. More important, the speed with which the camera moves calls attention to itself and makes it clear that the camera is responding directly to Lorne's commentary.

Through these interventions, Lorne's narration deliberately highlights the artificiality of the episode's construction by disturbing the seeming invisibility of storytelling and foregrounding the process of narration. In this manner Lorne stands in for Whedon himself as he is both storyteller and director. As a result, the episode serves as a stand-alone experiment in postmodern storytelling in which the process of telling a story is the story being told. Lorne's melancholic tone, however, also links the narration to the broader narrative arc of the episode and the season. His air of regret, which is increasingly apparent as the episode progresses, becomes all the more intense when the spell is reversed and the group, having lost their youthful innocence, are returned to their normal, adult selves with all of their tensions and emotional traumas restored. In split-screen composition, Lorne sits quietly at a piano playing a poignant tune as Wesley, Gunn, and Fred silently walk away in separate directions, visualizing their emotional isolation.

More significantly, Lorne's statement that "all's well that ends well—right kiddies? But since nothing ended all that well then I guess I gotta to say that nothing was well," spoken over an image of Cordelia as her memory is returned, contains dark implications for the end of the episode and the rest of the season. In this manner, Lorne's narration situates the episode clearly within the series' apocalyptic narrative, foreshadowing the horrors to come without revealing the form they will take. The final shot of Lorne leaving the stage and walking out through an empty bar closes the cabaret performance but leaves an open ending to the broader narrative. In this episode, therefore, Whedon's playful engagement with narrative construction serves as a self-contained experiment with storytelling as well as a dramatic primer for the rest of the season.

While "Are You Now or Have You Ever Been" and "Spin the Bottle" experiment with style and narrative, respectively, Ben Edlund's "Smile Time" extends the usual suspension of disbelief associated with the fantasy genre when the show's

Comedy becomes melodrama as Lorne narrates in "Spin the Bottle."

main hero, Angel, is turned into a puppet. This happens as Angel is investigating a children's TV program, *Smile Time,* after a number of children collapse in front of the television while watching the show, their faces frozen in wide-eyed grins. Through their investigation, Angel's team discover that the show's main characters, the puppets Polo, Flora, Groofus, and Horatio, are actually demons masquerading as puppets who are using the television signal to absorb the life forces of their juvenile audience. Through this narrative *Angel* consciously hybridizes the horror action series with children's television. The puppets are designed like the Muppets of *Sesame Street* (Children's Television Workshop/Sesame Workshop, 1969–), *The Muppet Show* (Associated Television, 1976–81), and *Fraggle Rock* (CBC, 1983–87), while the fictional show's programming style alludes to the educational intent of such Children's Television Workshop programs as *Sesame Street*, *The Electric Company* (CTW, 1971–77), and the long-running BBC series *Play School* (1964–88). This concept rivals Whedon's "Once More with Feeling" (*B*6:7)—

Buffy the Vampire Slayer's musical episode—for its generic daring. While both episodes operate under the precept that as stories located within a world of vampires, demons, and witches, much can be explained away as the result of a magic spell, replacing *Angel*'s lead actor David Boreanaz with a puppet for the majority of the episode is a hyperbolic extension of this fantasy narrative. The presence of the Angel-puppet, as well as locating the body of the story within a television studio, risks overtly reminding the audience of the series' construction and challenges what an audience can accept dramatically and generically. As such "Smile Time" walks a fine line between maintaining the integrity of its diegetic world by making the audience accept Angel's transformation into a puppet—and, more important, accept the puppet as Angel—and offering a satiric glance at the status of television and the representation of the superhero by this medium.

The process of making the puppet believable as Angel is achieved partly through the highly skilled work of the puppeteer (Drew Massey),[3] enhanced by the vocal performance of David Boreanaz, that mimics Angel's expressions and mannerisms perfectly. Its effectiveness is also due to the fact that the initial reaction of the other characters to Angel's condition mirrors the audience's, from the shocked expression of Wesley and Gunn to Fred's exclamation, "Oh my God. Angel, you're [pause—look of concern turns to a slight smile] cute." The episode repeatedly calls attention to our own disbelief and draws humor from the seeming ridiculousness of Angel's situation as well as his determination to continue in his position as action hero despite his condition. However, as the other characters engage with the puppet as Angel, the seeming incongruity of its presence dissipates.

In fact, the Angel-puppet becomes less of a disruption to the narrative when the demonic nature of *Smile Time*'s puppet stars—Polo, Flora, Groofus, and Horatio—is revealed. It is in the representation of these puppet demons that the episode's dark narrative merges with its satiric intent. These villains are in many ways the most disturbing monsters featured on *Angel*, largely because of the clear connotations of pedophilia inherent within their attack on the children. The episode opens with a young boy watching *Smile Time* as Polo, a puppet in the form of a young boy in dungarees and a baseball cap, waits until the boy's mother leaves the room, approaches the TV screen, and begins to speak to the boy directly, informing him that *Smile Time* isn't free and that he has to honor his promise. While he speaks with an innocent and friendly voice, it is clear that he is attempting to coerce the child, which is confirmed when his brow furrows and he angrily orders the boy to "Get over here and touch it." As the boy touches the TV screen, Polo, moaning with sexual pleasure, tells him, "That's it, Tommy. Touch it. That's it. . . . Good boy, Tommy," clearly conveying an "allusion to sexual abuse by a seemingly benign and trusted figure" (Abbott 2005a, 7).

At the same time the episode raises a familiar critique of the mind-numbing effects of television, when numerous children are found comatose while watching the program. It is later revealed that the TV demons are literally sucking the life out of the kids. This episode therefore serves as a culmination of a recurring and self-conscious critique of TV within *Angel*. For instance, in the episode "Belonging" (2:19), Cordelia, appearing in her first national commercial, is humiliated by a director who insults her and treats her as sexual prop to sell suntan lotion, conveying the insensitivity and self-importance of the director and the superficiality of the industry. This superficiality is also conveyed in the episode "Eternity" (1:17), which follows the AI team and their encounter with Rebecca Lowell, a television star so terrified of getting old and losing her celebrity status that she is willing to become a vampire in order to stay young forever. Finally in "Birthday" (3:11), an *It's a Wonderful Life*–style episode, Cordelia is offered a glimpse of an alternate life in which she did not meet Angel in L.A. and instead became a successful actress, star of her own sitcom, *Cordy*. While this episode has fun with the conventions of the sitcom primarily conveyed through the credit sequence that borrows heavily from the *Mary Tyler Moore Show* (1970–77) for its imagery, it is a gentle parody rather than a more harsh critique. It is, however, primarily through the sycophantic behavior of those dazzled by Cordy's star status that conveys the emptiness of TV stardom as contrasted with her more noble and worthwhile mission as a champion.

In "Smile Time," however, this critique of television becomes much more pointed and cynical. The image of the showrunner, Gregor Frampton (played by *Buffy*- and *Angel*-writer David Fury), turned into a human puppet, manipulated and tormented by the demons, serves as a convincing metaphor for the helplessness and frustration felt by TV creators in the face of the network. This message was particularly poignant at the time of airing on February 18, 2004, just five days after *Angel's* cancellation was announced. Furthermore, the episode also calls attention to the disparity between TV's commercial imperative and the aspirations for quality on behalf of its creators, as evidenced in this conversation between Polo and Groofus as they plan their final attack on their viewers.

> Groofus: So tomorrow's going to be a pretty big show, huh?
>
> Polo: The biggest!
>
> Groofus: Cool. Because I've been working on this great new song about the difference between analogy and metaphor . . .
>
> Polo: Man—are you out of your mind?
>
> Groofus: Well, we want it to be good, don't we?
>
> Polo: We EAT babies' lives!!!!
>
> Groofus: And uphold a certain standard of quality Edu-

tainment!

Polo: Screw Edutainment! [Shocked expression from the other puppets.] The life force we are pulling out of these snot-nosed kids is 100 percent pure innocence, dickwad. Do you have any idea of the street value that carries down in hell?!

That Groofus accepts the contradiction between eating "babies' lives" and upholding "standard[s] of quality Edutainment" conveys the irresolvable tension between creativity and commercialism inherent in quality television.

Finally, this episode also taps into the series' preoccupation, as discussed in chapter 2, with undermining conventional representations of masculinity and heroism through a critique of Angel's embodiment of the position of hero. This is partly achieved through the parody of the conventions of the superhero genre through the integration of the Angel-puppet within traditionally heroic set pieces, well established on the series. For instance, a recurring moment in most episodes in the series involves Angel heroically leading his team into action. This moment is made comic when, having realized that it is the puppet stars of TV's *Smile Time* who are attacking their young viewers, the Angel-puppet walks to the wall and dramatically removes a broad sword from its scabbard as he commands, "Well, then, let's take out some puppets!" The comedy is punctuated by a cut to a medium long shot of the door to Angel's office as it is pulled opened by Fred, followed by Wesley and Gunn, as the camera cranes down to reveal the Angel-puppet, broadsword in hand, leading the way.

Positioning the puppet literally at the head of the team, photographed in slow motion and accompanied by a swell of commanding music, comically lampoons the conventions of the show itself. Similarly, the battle on the *Smile Time* set, during a live broadcast, parodies the traditional *Angel* fight

"Wee little puppet man" leads the fight in "Smile Time."

scenes through the violent interplay between our heroes and their foes as Gunn dismembers two of the puppets while the Angel-puppet throttles another. This is truly unconventional programming for both *Angel* and kids' TV.

Furthermore, the episode's parody extends to Angel's crisis in masculinity for, as Roz Kaveney points out, "Angel's constant sense of his bad faith is reinforced by various things that happen to him in the course of the [fifth] season" that undermine his status as a champion and as a man. "In the course of Season Five, he is magically compelled to have sex with the Senior Partners' minion, confronted with the apparent meaninglessness of another hero's struggles, poisoned by a demon parasite into endless hallucinations of his own worthlessness and finally literally reduced to the status of a puppet" (2005, 62–63). As a puppet, Angel, the dark, mysterious, and handsome hero, is the object of much humor as he is humiliated by his new appearance, preferring to hide under his desk rather than be seen by Nina, his prospective werewolf-girlfriend, and reduced to the status of "cute" as Fred gushes over his "little hands" and tousles his spiked-up hair. His humiliation is compounded by Spike's mocking remarks as he describes Angel as a "wee little puppet man."

This humiliation extends to vulnerability, both emotional and physical, when Angel finally reveals his condition to Nina, who is locked in a cage as she prepares for her monthly transformation. Here he shows his resignation with his condition by responding to her concern with "I'm made of felt and my nose comes off." Furthermore, as he opens up to Nina about his own insecurities with himself as well as his inability to engage with the world around him, echoing a conversation he had had with Wesley in his non-puppet form at the beginning of the episode, Nina, now fully transformed into a werewolf, attacks him, ripping his felt body to shreds. Lorne later finds Angel as he collapses in the office corridor, holding in his stuffing as though it were his intestines. Angel's degradation is complete as his werewolf-girlfriend tries to eat him. The episode ends with Angel still in puppet form, but he is told that his condition is improving, concluding not with normality—along with his masculinity and strength—restored but with Angel accepting his vulnerability as a part of himself as he takes Nina (the werewolf who tried to eat him) out for breakfast. The image of the Angel-puppet walking hand in hand with the tall, sexy blonde comically and quietly undermines the romance of the moment. Each of the episodes discussed in this chapter demonstrates how the show often engages in sometimes playful and sometimes serious experimentation with the televisual form and yet these experiments continued to serve the broader narrative and character arcs of the show. They also drive home one of the show's primary themes, which was to reimagine the nature of heroism, either through parody or by drawing attention to Angel's morally ambiguous nature.

When considered together, these three episodes—"Are You Now or Have You Ever Been," "Spin the Bottle," and "Smile Time"—each written by a different person but produced within the culture of collective creativity discussed in chapter 1, serve as exemplary case studies of the series creators' preoccupation with exploring complex notions of masculinity, defying conventional understandings of genre, and developing a richly textured visual aesthetic that distinguishes it from other fantasy series as discussed throughout this book. They also demonstrate how Joss Whedon and his team of writers, directors, and actors saw that looking at the world through the morally and emotionally complex gaze of a vampire with a soul offered a unique and enlightening perspective on the darkness and light of the world around us. Angel tells Connor, "We live as if the world were as it should be to show it what it can be" ("Deep Down," 4:1). In this manner, *Angel* proved itself to be more than simply a spin-off from *Buffy the Vampire Slayer* but instead offered its own vision, developed its own style, fostered its own fandom, and carved for itself a place in traditions of the horror and superhero genres on television.

Introduction

"Eternity" (1:17).

1. See Schneider and Adalian 2001.
2. While the overall budget actually stayed the same, increases in the cast's salaries as well as the addition of James Marsters's salary meant that the production budget of the series had been effectively reduced (Gross 2003a, 58).
3. The *Law and Order* spin-offs are *Law and Order: Special Victims Unit* (1999–), *Law and Order: Criminal Intent* (2001–), and *Law and Order: Trial by Jury* (2005).

Chapter 1

This is the sound used to accompany the Mutant Enemy monster logo.

1. The term *broken* here refers to the process of mapping out the story for an individual episode and breaking it down into its four act structure. For an illustration of how this process works, see Minear 2006, in which Minear runs a seminar on how to break an episode of *Angel*.
2. I should stress that in this context I am specifically discussing the role of the writer in American television and must acknowledge that the writer does not necessarily play the same role in television in other countries.

3. While not a major American network, the WB was a smaller net-let that relied on advertising income and based its season struc-ture on the twenty-two- to twenty-four-episode season common to major networks like ABC, CBC, and NBC. This is quite unlike the pay channel HBO, which is subscription based and encour-ages experimentation within its series as a marker of the quality around which it has based its reputation. Furthermore, HBO se-ries usually contain twelve episodes a season, a structure that re-lieves the production pressure on the writers, cast, and crew that is often experienced by those involved in series broadcast on com-mercial networks.

4. Much of the information about the writing process was gained from a wide range of interviews with many of the writers at Mutant Enemy available at http://www.cityofangel.com, as well as interviews with David Greenwalt and Joss Whedon printed in Nazzaro 2002, and interviews with Steven DeKnight and Jane Es-penson printed in Kaveney 2004b. Other useful sources on this subject include Jane Espenson's blog, www.janeespenson.com; Tim Minear's website, www.TimMinear.net; Minear 2006; and Whedon 2005a.

5. For a broader discussion of sex and violence in relation to Faith, see Tjardes (2003).

Chapter 2

"Billy" (3:6).

1. This color is also used in the seventh season of *Buffy the Vampire Slayer* in relation to the return of Spike's soul in the episode "Be-neath You" (7:2) (see Abbott 2005b, 337–38, for a further discus-sion of this).

2. As Jason Mittell argues, integrating genres does not necessarily diffuse their individual meaning but "brings generic practices to the surface, making the conventions and assumptions clustered within individual categories explicit through the juxtaposition of conflicting or complementary genres" (2004, 157).

3. This can be the case with film as well. For instance, the film *Scream* (Wes Craven, 1996) effectively parodies the conventions of the slasher film while also operating as a scary horror movie.

Chapter 3

"Sense and Sensitivity" (1:6).

1. When broadcast on January 11, 1972, *The Night Stalker*, with seventy-five million viewers, had the "biggest audience to that date for a television film" (Roeger 1979, 39).

2. My thanks to Lorna Jowett for reminding me of this statement by Chris Carter.

3. *Saw* (James Wan, 2004); *Saw II* (Darren Lynn Bousman, 2005); *Saw III* (Darren Lynn Bousman, 2006); *Saw IV* (Darren Lynn Bousman, 2007); *Hostel* (Eli Roth, 2005); *Hostel II* (Eli Roth, 2007).

4. This episode was just one of the many casualties of Channel Four's attempt to make *Angel* suitable for this time slot. Episodes "City Of" and "Rm w/a Vu" were also severely cut while "Somnambulist," "Expecting," and "I've Got You under My Skin" were never aired because they were deemed to be unsuitable for the family audience being targeted in this time slot (Hill and Calcutt, 2001). For a more detailed discussion of the broadcast of *Buffy* and *Angel* in the United Kingdom, see Hill and Calcutt.

5. Andrew Tudor defines an "unruly body" as a body that is both under attack from an internal threat but is also itself threatening (1995, 27).

6. Lorna Jowett has argued that Angel's "suffering [physical, psychological, and emotional] becomes an assertion of masculinity," but at the same time the representation of Angel's body on the series positions his masculinity as "openly contested" (2004).

Chapter 4

1. The series' preoccupation with masculinity is demonstrated by the numerous articles and conference papers that have focused on this aspect of the show. See in particular Jowett 2004; Bradley 2005; Beeler 2005; Meyer 2005; and Davis 2004.

2. The relationship between Wesley and Gunn, formed when Angel fires the team and the two men, along with Cordelia, establish their own agency, is worth further analysis in terms of traditional male bonding rituals, in this case demon-hunting, the transgression of class and racial boundaries, and the role of the love triangle in representations of male friendship.

3. My thanks to Ann Fraser for her insight into *Starsky and Hutch* and for recommending these episodes in particular as key moments in the partners' friendship.

Chapter 5

"Judgment" (2:1).

1. For further discussion of the links between *Angel* and aesthetic experimentation, see Kinsey 2005, which looks at how the transition sequences and psychic visions displayed in the series draw on traditions of experimental cinema.

2. Numerous other moments in the episode further emphasize these themes of paranoia, prejudice, and fear, such as the Hollywood actor who, fearing discovery by the studio, uses the hotel as the clandestine site for his homosexual encounters, the prostitute who uses the hotel for her own professional activities, and the African American family who are refused a room in the hotel and are told that "the sign was wrong. There are no vacancies."

3. Massey has worked as a puppeteer on *Muppets Tonight* (ABC, 1996–98), *It's a Very Merry Muppet Christmas Movie* (Kirk R. Thatcher, 2002), *Crank Yankers* (Comedy Central, 2003), and *Eminem's Making the Ass* (MTV, 2005).

Abbott, Stacey. 2001. A Little Less Ritual and a Little More Fun: The Modern Vampire in *Buffy the Vampire Slayer*. *Slayage: The Online International Journal of Buffy Studies* 3 (June), www.slayageon-line.com/essays/slayage3/sabbott.htm.

———. 2003. Walking the Fine Line between Angel and Angelus. *Slayage: The Online International Journal of Buffy Studies* 9 (August), www.slayageonline.com/essays/slayage9/Abbott.htm.

———. 2005a. Kicking Ass and Singing "Mandy": A Vampire in L.A. In *Reading "Angel": The TV Spin-off with a Soul*, ed. Stacey Abbott, 1–13. London: I. B. Tauris.

———. 2005b. From Madman in the Basement to Self-Sacrificing Champion: The Multiple Faces of Spike. *European Journal of Cultural Studies* 8, no. 3: 329–44.

———. 2007. *Celluloid Vampires: Life after Death in the Modern World*. Austin: University of Texas Press.

Amy-Chinn, Dee. 2005. Queering the Bitch: Spike, Transgression and Erotic Empowerment. *European Journal of Cultural Studies* 8, no. 3: 313–28.

Beeler, Stan. 2005. Outing Lorne: Performance for the Performers. In *Reading "Angel": The TV Spin-off with a Soul*, ed. Stacey Abbott, 88–100. London: I. B. Tauris.

Berger, Maurice, Brian Wallis, and Simon Watson, eds. 1995. *Constructing Masculinity*. London: Routledge.

Bianculli, David. 1999. Old Pals Stake out Their New Turf. *Daily News N.Y.*, October 5: 74.

Bradley, Catherine. 2005. Men in Mayhem, Men in Masquerade: An Enquiry into the Representations of Angel and Wesley in "Guise Will Be Guise." Paper presented at "'Bring Your Own Subtext': Social Life, Human Experience, and the Works of Joss Whedon" conference. University of Huddersfield, June 29–July 1.

Bratton, Kristy. 2000. Behind the Scenes: Featuring Tim Minear: Writer/Producer for *Angel*. City of Angel, www.cityofangel.com/behindTheScenes/bts/minear1.html (accessed July 7, 2006).

———. 2002. The Grass Is Always Greeny-er: An Exclusive Spotlight on David Greenwalt. City of Angel, www.cityofangel.com/behindTheScenes/bts2/greenySpot.html (accessed July 5, 2006).

Brophy, Philip. 1986. Horrality—The Textuality of Contemporary Horror Films. *Screen* 27, no. 1: 2–13.

Butler, Judith. 1990. *Gender Trouble: The Subversion of Identity*. New York: Routledge.

Calvert, Bronwen. 2007. "This Shell I'm In": Monstrous Embodiment and the Case of Illyria in *Angel*. Paper presented at "*Buffy* Hereafter: From the Whedonverse to the Whedonesque: An Interdisciplinary Conference on the Works of Joss Whedon and Its Aftereffects." Istanbul, October 17–19.

Carroll, Noël. 1990. *The Philosophy of Horror: Or Paradoxes of the Heart*. New York: Routledge.

Colvin, Phil. 2005. *Angel*: Redefinition and Justification through Faith. In *Reading "Angel": The TV Spin-off with a Soul*, ed. Stacey Abbott, 17–30. London: I. B. Tauris.

Creed, Barbara. 1993. *The Monstrous-Feminine: Film, Feminism, Psychoanalysis*. London: Routledge.

———. 1995. Horror and the Carnivalesque: The Body-Monstrous. In *Fields of Vision: Essays in Film Studies, Visual Anthropology, and Photography*, ed. Leslie Devereaux and Roger Hillman, 127–59. Berkeley: University of California Press.

Davis, Peggy. 2004. "I'm a Rogue Demon-Hunter": Wesley's Transformation from Fop to Hero on *Buffy the Vampire Slayer* and *Angel*. Paper presented at the Slayage Conference on Buffy the Vampire Slayer. Nashville, May 27–30.

DiLullo, Tara. 2003. Inside Out: An Exclusive Interview with Writer Steven S. DeKnight. City of Angel, www.cityofangel.com/behindTheScenes/bts3/deKnight.html (accessed March 7, 2003).

Elsaesser, Thomas. 1987. Tales of Sound and Fury: Observations on the Family Melodrama. In *Home Is Where the Heart Is: Studies in Melodrama and the Woman's Film*, ed. Christine Gledhill, 43–69. London: BFI.

Espenson, Jane. 2003. Introduction to *Slayer Slang: A "Buffy the Vampire Slayer" Lexicon*, by Michael Adams, vii–x. Oxford: Oxford University Press.

Faludi, Susan. 2000. *Stiffed: The Betrayal of Modern Man*. London: Vintage.

Feuer, Jane. 1992. Genre and Television. In *Channels of Discourse, Reassembled: Television and Contemporary Criticism*, ed. R. Allen. London: Routledge.

Frank, Micheline Klagsbrun. 1990. Unchained: Perspectives on Change. *Journal of Popular Film and Television* 18, no. 3: 122–29.

Fuchs, Cynthia J. 1993. The Buddy Politic. In *Screening the Male: Exploring Masculinities in Hollywood Cinema*, ed. Steven Cohan and Ina Rae Hark, 194–210. London: Routledge.

Greenwalt, David. 2003. From Page to Screen. Featurette. *"Angel" Season Three DVD Collection*, Region 2, Twentieth Century Fox.

Greppi, Michele. 1999. The Trouble with an *Angel*. *New York Post* October 5: 98.

Gross, Edward. 2000a. Angel: Season One, Episode by Episode with Tim Minear—Part 3. Originally appearing in fandom.com, reprinted on TimMinear.net., www.timminear.net/archives/angel/000041.html (accessed August 29, 2006).

———. 2000b. Angel: Season One, Episode by Episode with Tim Minear—Part 4. Originally appearing in fandom.com, reprinted on TimMinear.net. www.timminear.net/archives/angel/000042.html (accessed August 29, 2006).

———. 2003a. Angel Evolutions. *Cinefantastique* 35, no. 5: 54–59.

———. 2003b. Spike Everlasting. *Cinefantastique* 35, no. 5: 57.

Halfyard, Janet K. 2005. The Dark Avenger: Angel and the Cinematic Superhero. In *Reading "Angel": The TV Spin-off with a Soul*, ed. Stacey Abbott, 149–62. London: I. B. Tauris.

Hill, Annette, and Ian Calcutt. 2001. Vampire Hunters: The Scheduling and Reception of *Buffy the Vampire Slayer* and *Angel* in the UK. *Intensities: The Journal of Cult Media* no. 1, http://davidlavery.net/Intensities/Intensitites_1.htm (accessed October 8, 2007).

Hills, Matt. 2005. *Pleasures of Horror*. London: Continuum.

Hills, Matt, and Rebecca Williams. 2005. *Angel*'s Monstrous Mothers

111

and Vampires with Souls: Investigating the Abject in Television Horror. In *Reading "Angel": The TV Spin-off with a Soul*, ed. Stacey Abbott, 203–17. London: I. B. Tauris.

Hudson, Jennifer A. 2005. "She's Unpredictable": Illyria and the Liberating Potential of Chaotic Postmodern Identity. *American Popular Culture,* www.americanpopularculture.com/archive/tv/shes_unpredictable.htm (accessed July 4, 2005).

Jacob, Benjamin. 2005. Los Angelus: The City of Angel. In *Reading "Angel": The TV Spin-off with a Soul*, ed. Stacey Abbott, 75–87. London: I. B. Tauris.

Jacobs, Jason. 2003. *Body Trauma TV: The New Hospital Dramas*. London: BFI.

Jancovich, Mark, and Nathan Hunt. 2004. The Mainstream, Distinction, and Cult TV. In *Cult Television*, ed. Sara Gwenllian-Jones and Roberta E. Pearson, 27–44. Minneapolis: University of Minnesota Press.

Jeffords, Susan. 1993. Can Masculinity Be Terminated? In *Screening the Male: Exploring Masculinities in Hollywood Cinema*, ed. Steven Cohan and Ina Rae Hark, 245–62. London: Routledge.

Jermyn, Deborah. 2007. Body Matters: Realism, Spectacle and the Corpse in *CSI*. In *Reading CSI*, ed. Mike Allen. London: I. B. Tauris.

Johnson, Catherine. 2005. *Telefantasy*. London: BFI.

Jowett, Lorna. 2004. Not Like Other Men? The Male Body and Masculinities in *Angel*. Unpublished paper.

———. 2005. *Sex and the Slayer: A Gender Studies Primer for the Buffy Fan*. Middletown, CT: Wesleyan University Press.

Kaveney, Roz. 2004a. She Saved the World a Lot: An Introduction to the Themes and Structures of *Buffy* and *Angel*. In *Reading the Vampire Slayer: The New Updated Unofficial Guide to Buffy and Angel*, ed. Roz Kaveney, 1–82. London: I. B. Tauris.

———. 2004b. Writing the Vampire Slayer: Interviews with Jane Espenson and Steven S. DeKnight. In *Reading the Vampire Slayer: The New Updated Unofficial Guide to Buffy and Angel*, ed. Roz Kaveney, 100–131. London: I. B. Tauris.

———. 2005. A Sense of the Ending: Schrodinger's Angel. In *Reading "Angel": The TV Spin-Off with a Soul*, ed. Stacey Abbott, 57–72. London: I. B. Tauris.

Kinsey, Tammy A. 2005. Transitions and Time: The Cinematic Language of *Angel*. In *Reading "Angel": The TV Spin-Off with a Soul*, ed.

Stacey Abbott, 44–56. London: I. B. Tauris.

Kitman, Marvin. 1999. Only Suckers Will Sink Their Teeth into *Angel*. *Newsday*, October 4: B23.

Kouf, Jim. 2001. Five by Five. Script. *"Angel" Season One DVD Collection*, Region 2, Twentieth Century Fox.

Kristeva, Julia. 1982. *Powers of Horror: An Essay on Abjection*. Trans. Leon S. Roudiez. New York: Columbia University Press.

Lavery, David. 2002. Afterword: The Genius of Joss Whedon. In *Fighting the Forces: What's at Stake in "Buffy the Vampire Slayer,"* ed. Rhonda V. Wilcox and David Lavery, 251–56. Lanham, MD: Rowman and Littlefield.

Malcolm, Shawna. 2002. Angel Bites Back. *TV Guide*, May 4: 55–58.

———. 2004. Interview with the Vampires. *TV Guide,* January 31: 22–24.

Mauceri, Joe. 2000. Diabolical Mastermind. *Shivers* no. 76 (April): 8–10.

Meyer, Michaela D. E. 2005. From Rogue in the 'Hood to Suave in a Suit: Black Masculinity and the Transformation of Charles Gunn. In *Reading "Angel": The TV Spin-off with a Soul*, ed. Stacey Abbott, 176–88. London: I. B. Tauris.

Millman, Joyce. 2001. Lessons in Being Human. *New York Times* (Sunday), September 23: 21, 30.

Minear, Tim. 2002. Are You Now or Have You Ever Been. Commentary. *"Angel" Season Two DVD Collection*, Region 2, Twentieth Century Fox.

———. 2006. *Screenwriting Expo Seminar Series #046: Breaking the Story*. CS Publications. DVD, Region 1.

Minear, Tim, and Jeffrey Bell. 2003. Billy. Commentary. *"Angel" Season Three DVD Collection*, Region 2, Twentieth Century Fox.

Minear, Tim, and Joss Whedon. 2001. Sanctuary. Script. *"Angel" Season One DVD Collection*, Region 2, Twentieth Century Fox.

Mittell, Jason. 2004. *Genre and Television: From Cop Shows to Cartoons in American Culture*. New York: Routledge.

Nazzaro, Joe. 2002. *Writing Science Fiction and Fantasy Television*. London: Titan Books.

———. 2003. Creatures of DeKnight. *TV Zone* no. 167 (September): 52–57.

Neale, Steve, and Frank Krutnik. 1990. *Popular Film and Television Comedy*. London: Routledge.

Parks, Steve. 1999. *Roswell* Has More Bite Than *Angel*. *Newsday,* Octo-

113

ber 3–9: 3.

Pearson, Roberta. 2005. The Writer/Producer in American Television. In *The Contemporary Television Series*, ed. Michael Hammond and Lucy Mazdon, 11–26. Edinburgh: Edinburgh University Press.

Persons, Mitch. 1999. Angel, Vampire Private Eye. *Cinefantastique* 31, no. 8: 10–11.

Prawer, S. S. 1980. *Caligari's Children: The Film as Tale of Terror*. New York: Oxford University Press.

Robinson, Sally. 2000. *Marked Men: White Masculinity in Crisis*. New York: Columbia University Press.

Roeger, Berthe. 1979. *Kolchak: The Night Stalker*: The Family-Hour Fiend-Fest That Became a Late-Night Sensation. *Fangoria* 3: 39–40.

Roush, Matt. 1999. New to L.A.: Cool Ghouls. *TV Guide,* November 13: 16.

Sayer, Karen. 2004. This Was Our World and They Made It Theirs: Reading Space and Place in *Buffy the Vampire Slayer* and *Angel*. In *Reading the Vampire Slayer: The New Updated Unofficial Guide to Buffy and Angel*, ed. Roz Kaveney, 132–55. London: I. B. Tauris.

Schneider, Michael, and Josef Adalian. 2001. Studio Sibs Fuel Renewals: Battle over *Buffy* Puts Mega-congloms' Might on Display. *Variety* 15 (January): 41–42.

Sedgwick, Eve. 1985. *Between Men: English Literature and Male Homosocial Desire*. New York: Columbia University Press.

Shamir, Milette, and Jennifer Travis. 2002. Introduction to *Boys Don't Cry: Rethinking Narratives of Masculinity and Emotion in the U.S.,* ed. Milette Shamir and Jennifer Travis, 1–21. New York: Columbia University Press.

Smith, Mere. 2003. From Page to Screen. Featurette. *"Angel" Season Three DVD Collection*, Region 2, Twentieth Century Fox.

Spangler, Lynn C. 1992. Buddies and Pals: A History of Male Friendships on Prime-Time Television. In *Men, Masculinity and the Media*, ed. Steve Craig, 93–110. London: Sage.

Stoy, Jennifer. 2005. "And Her Tears Flowed Like Wine": Wesley/Lilah and the Complicated (?) Role of the Female Agent on *Angel*. In *Reading "Angel": The TV Spin-Off with a Soul*, ed. Stacey Abbott, 163–75. London: I. B. Tauris.

Thompson, Robert J. 1996. *Television's Second Golden Age: From "Hill Street Blues" to "ER."* Syracuse: Syracuse University Press.

Tjardes, Sue. 2003. "If You're Not Enjoying It, You're Doing Something

Wrong": Textual and Viewer Constructions of Faith, the Vampire Slayer. In *Athena's Daughters: Television's New Women Warriors*, ed. Frances Early and Kathleen Kennedy, 66–77. Syracuse: Syracuse University Press.

Tudor, Andrew. 1995. Unruly Bodies, Unquiet Minds. *Body and Society* no. 1 (March): 25–41.

Turner, Graeme. 2001. Genre, Hybridity and Mutation. In *The Television Genre Book*, ed. Glen Creeber, 6–7. London: BFI.

Waller, Gregory A. 1987a. Introduction to *American Horrors: Essays on the Modern American Horror Film*, ed. Gregory A. Waller, 1–13. Urbana: University of Illinois Press.

———. 1987b. Made-for-Television Horror Films. In *American Horrors: Essays on the Modern American Horror Film*, ed. Gregory A. Waller, 145–61. Urbana: University of Illinois Press.

Werts, Diane. 1999. *Angel* Sinks Fangs in WB. *Newsday,* October 5: B31.

Wheatley, Helen. 2006. *Gothic Television*. Manchester: Manchester University Press.

Whedon, Joss. 2001. City Of. Commentary. *"Angel" Season One DVD Collection,* Region 2, Twentieth Century Fox.

———. 2005a. *Creative Screenwriting Presents: Joss Whedon: The Master at Play.* CS Publications. DVD, Region 1.

———. 2005b. A Hole in the World. Commentary. *"Angel" Season Five DVD Collection*, Region 2, Twentieth Century Fox.

Wilcox, Rhonda V. 2005. *Why Buffy Matters: The Art of "Buffy the Vampire Slayer."* London: I. B. Tauris.

Wilcox, Rhonda V., and David Lavery. 2005. Afterword: The Depths of *Angel* and the Birth of *Angel* Studies. In *Reading "Angel": The TV Spin-Off with a Soul*, ed. Stacey Abbott, 221–29. London: I. B. Tauris.

Wood, Robin. 1986. *Hollywood from Vietnam to Reagan*. New York: Columbia University Press.

115